iPhone®

PORTABLE GENIUS

SIXTH EDITION

Paul McFedries

WILEY

SKY10022529_111320

Published simultaneously in Canada

ISBN: 978-1-119-76362-8
ISBN: 978-1-119-76509-7 (ebk)
ISBN: 978-1-119-76363-5 (ebk)

Manufactured in the United States of America

For general information on our other products and services please contact our Customer Care Department within the United States at (877) 762-2974, outside the United States at (317) 572-3993 or fax (317) 572-4002.

Wiley publishes in a variety of print and electronic formats and by print-on-demand. Some material included with standard print versions of this book may not be included in e-books or in print-on-demand. If this book refers to media such as a CD or DVD that is not included in the version you purchased, you may download this material at booksupport.wiley.com. For more information about Wiley products, visit www.wiley.com.

Library of Congress Control Number: 2020949809

This book is dedicated to my beautiful wife, Karen,
who is wise, funny, and smart, even in texts.

About the Author

Paul McFedries is a full-time technical writer. Paul has been authoring computer books since 1991 and has nearly 100 books to his credit. Paul's books have sold more than four million copies worldwide. These books include the Wiley titles *Windows Portable Genius; iPad Portable Genius,* Fourth Edition; *Teach Yourself VISUALLY Windows 10,* Third Edition; and *G Suite for Dummies*. You can visit Paul on the web at www.mcfedries.com or on Twitter at www.twitter.com/paulmcf.

Acknowledgments

I had a great time writing this book because it's just pure fun to write about what's new and noteworthy in the iPhone, particularly the lesser-known features that can make your life easier and more efficient. More than that, however, I got to work with a great bunch of professionals at Wiley. There's a long list of people who contributed to the making of this book, and I extend a hearty thanks to all of them for their hard work and competence. A few of those people I had the pleasure of working with directly included Associate Publisher Jim Minatel, Project Editors Maureen and Scott Tullis, Copy Editor Kim Wimpsett, and Content Refinement Specialist Barath Kumar Rajasekaran. Many thanks to each of you for the skill, professionalism, sense of humor, and general niceness that made my job infinitely easier and made this a better book.

Contents

chapter 3

chapter 4

chapter 5

chapter 6

chapter 7

chapter 8

Introduction

The iPhone is a success not because more than 2 billion of them have been sold (or, I should say, not *only* because over 2 billion of them have been sold; that's a *lot* of phones!), but because the iPhone has reached the status of a cultural icon. Even people who don't care much for gadgets in general and cell phones in particular know about the iPhone. For those of us who do care about gadgets, the iPhone elicits a kind of technological longing that can be satisfied in only one way: by buying one.

Part of the iconic status of the iPhone comes from its gorgeous design and remarkable interface, which makes all the standard tasks — surfing, emailing, texting, scheduling, and playing — easy and intuitive. But just as an attractive face or an easygoing manner can hide a personality of complexity and depth, so too does the iPhone hide many of its most useful and interesting features.

When you want to get beyond the basics of iPhone and solve some of its riddles, you might know some iPhone geniuses in person or online. Ideally, you'll get good advice on how to get your iPhone to do what you want it to do. Asking a genius is a great thing, but it isn't always a convenient thing because geniuses often have better things to do with their time.

What you really need is a "genius" of your own that's easier to access, more convenient, and doesn't require pleading emails or bribery. What you really need is a portable genius that enables you to be more productive and solve problems — wherever you and your iPhone happen to be.

Welcome, therefore, to *iPhone Portable Genius,* Sixth Edition. This book is kind of a genius all wrapped up in an easy-to-use, easy-to-access, and eminently portable format. In this book, you learn how to get more out of your iPhone by accessing all the powerful and timesaving features that aren't obvious at a casual glance. In this book, you learn about all the amazing new features found in the latest iPhones and the latest version of iOS. In this book, you learn how to prevent iPhone problems from occurring and (just in case your preventative measures are for naught) how to fix many common problems.

This book is for iPhone users who know the basics but want to take their iPhone education to a higher level. It's a book for people who want to be more productive, more efficient, more creative, and more self-sufficient (at least as far as the iPhone goes). It's a book for people who use their iPhone every day but would like to incorporate it into more of their day-to-day activities. It's a book I had a blast writing, so I think it's a book you'll enjoy reading.

How Do I Start Using My iPhone?

1 2 3 4 5 6 7 8 9 10 11

When you first look at your iPhone, you notice its sleek, curvaceous design, and then you notice what might be its most remarkable feature: It's nearly button-free! Unlike your garden-variety smartphone bristling with keys and switches and ports, your iPhone has very few physical buttons. This makes for a stylish, possibly even sexy, design, but it also leads to an obvious problem out of the box: How do you work the darn thing? This chapter solves that problem by giving you the grand tour of your iPhone. You learn about the few physical buttons on the phone, and then I show you the real heart of the iPhone, the remarkable touchscreen.

Working with the Side Button

If your iPhone is on but you're not using it, the phone automatically goes into standby mode after one minute. This is called Auto-Lock, and it's a handy feature because it saves battery power when your iPhone is just sitting there. However, you can also put your iPhone into standby mode at any time by using the Side button (also called the Sleep/Wake button). As pointed out in Figure 1.1, you find this button on the right side of your phone, assuming you're holding the phone as shown in Figure 1.1 (this is called *portrait* orientation). (On older iPhones, the Side button is on the top of your phone.)

1.1 On all recent iPhone models, the Side button appears on the right side.

As I describe in the following sections, the Side button has four main functions: sleeping and waking, powering on and off, handling incoming calls, and authorizing purchases.

Sleeping and waking the iPhone

If you're currently using your iPhone, you put the phone in standby mode by pressing the Side button once. You can still receive incoming calls and texts, but the screen powers down, which drops the power consumption considerably. Tap the Side button again to wake your iPhone (or just tap the screen). You're prompted with the Swipe Up to Open message shown in Figure 1.1, and you slide your finger up from the bottom of the screen to unlock the phone (or enter your passcode).

Genius

Press the Side button to put your phone in standby whenever you're not using the screen. This not only conserves battery power but also prevents accidental screen taps. If you have a program such as the Music app running, it continues to run even while the phone is in standby.

Powering the iPhone on and off

You can also use the Side button to turn off your iPhone so that it uses no power. This is a good idea if your battery is getting low and you don't think you'll be able to charge it any time soon. You can still periodically check your messages or make an outgoing call when needed, but as long as you turn off the phone when you're done, you minimize the chance that your battery will drain completely. You might also want to turn off your iPhone if you won't be using it for a few days.

Follow these steps to turn off your iPhone:

1. **Press and hold both the Side button and either the Volume Up or Volume Down button (pointed out in Figure 1.1) for a couple of seconds.** The Slide to Power Off slider appears on the screen, as shown in Figure 1.2. For the record, note that this screen also comes with three other features of note:

   - **Medical ID.** Drag this slider all the way to the right to open the Medical ID page, which shows your name, your date of birth, and your medical conditions, allergies, medications, blood type, and more. To configure your Medical ID page, open Settings, tap Health, and then tap Medical ID.

   - **Emergency SOS.** Drag this slider all the way to the right to place a call to your local emergency service (such as 911) and, once the call ends, to optionally send an emergency text to each person listed in the Health app's Emergency Contacts list. To configure Emergency SOS, open Settings and tap Emergency SOS.

- **Cancel.** Tap this button if you change your mind and decide to leave your iPhone on.

2. **Use your finger to drag Slide to Power Off all the way to the right.** The iPhone shuts down after a few seconds.

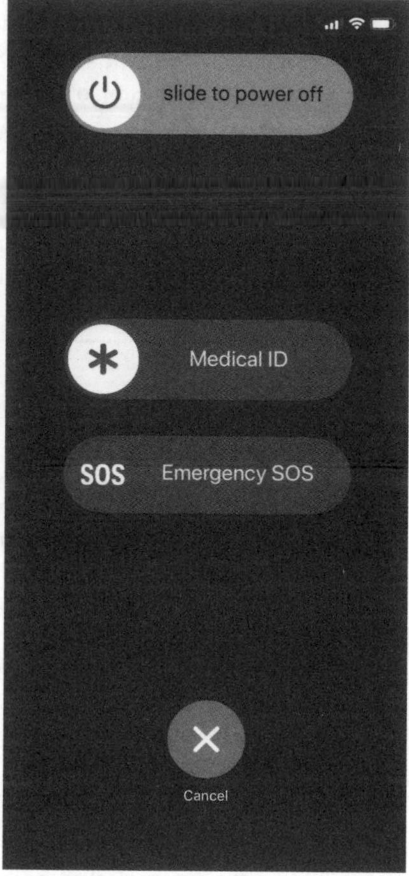

1.2 Press and hold the Side button and a Volume button to display this screen.

When you're ready to resume your iPhone chores, press and hold the Side button until you see the Apple icon. The iPhone powers up and then a few seconds later displays the unlock screen.

Silencing or declining a call

The Side button has another couple of tricks up its electronic sleeve, and these features give you quick ways to handle incoming calls:

- **Silence an incoming call.** Press the Side button once. This temporarily turns off the ringer, which is great in situations where you don't want to disturb the folks around you. You still have the standard four rings to answer, should you decide to. If you don't answer, your iPhone sends the call to your voicemail.
- **Decline an incoming call.** Press the Side button twice. This sends the call directly to voicemail, which is useful in situations where you don't want the ringing to disturb your neighbors and you don't want to answer the call. Note that, in this case, you don't have the option of answering the call.

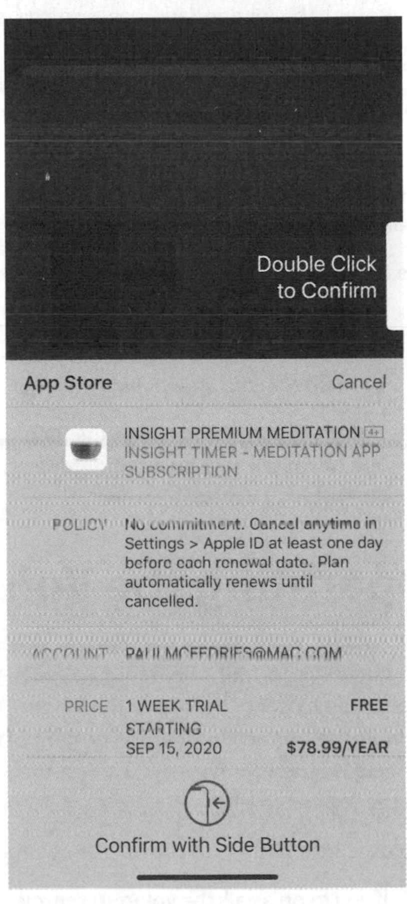

1.3 Double-click the Side button to authorize an app or in-app purchase.

Making a purchase

If your iPhone has Face ID, you also use the Side button to make purchases:

- **Use Apple Pay in a store.** Double-click the Side button to use your default Apple Pay card. For more about Face ID and setting up Apple Pay, see Chapter 2.
- **Confirm an app or in-app purchase.** Wait until you see the Double Click to Confirm prompt shown in Figure 1.3; then double-click the Side button to authorize the purchase.

Working with the Ring/Silent Switch

When a call comes in and you press the Side button once, your iPhone silences the ringer. That's great if you're in a meeting or a movie, but the only problem is that it may take you one or two rings before you can tap the Side button, and by that time the folks nearby are already glaring at you.

To prevent this phone faux pas, you can switch your iPhone into Silent Mode, which means it doesn't ring, and it doesn't play any alerts or sound effects. When the sound is turned off, only alarms that you've set using the Clock application will sound. The phone will still vibrate unless you turn this feature off as well.

You switch the iPhone between Ring Mode and Silent Mode using the Ring/Silent switch, which is located on the left side of the iPhone, near the top (assuming you're holding the phone in portrait orientation), as shown earlier in Figure 1.1.

Use the following techniques to switch between Silent Mode and Ring Mode:

- **Put the phone in Silent Mode.** Flick the Ring/Silent switch toward the back of the phone. You see an orange stripe on the switch, the iPhone vibrates briefly, and you see a brief notification telling you that Silent Mode is on.
- **Return to Ring Mode.** Flick the Ring/Silent switch toward the front of the phone. You no longer see the orange stripe on the switch, and the iPhone displays the current ringer volume setting.

Operating the Volume Controls

The volume controls are on the left side of the iPhone (again, when you're holding the phone in portrait orientation), right below the Ring/Silent switch (see Figure 1.1). The button closer to the top of the iPhone is Volume Up, and you press it to increase the volume; the button closer to the bottom of the iPhone is Volume Down, and you press it to decrease the volume. As you adjust the volume, a slider appears on-screen representing the volume level.

You use these buttons to control the volume throughout your iPhone:

- If you're on a call, the volume controls adjust your speaker volume.
- If you're using the Music app, the volume controls adjust the music volume.
- In all other situations, the volume controls adjust the output of sounds such as alerts and effects.

Inserting a SIM Card

Before you can use your iPhone to make and receive calls over the cellular network, you need to insert a SIM (subscriber identity module) card, which your cellular provider includes with your phone (or which you can purchase separately as a prepaid card).

With your SIM card at hand, follow these steps to insert it into your iPhone:

1. **Locate the SIM removal tool that came with your phone.** Figure 1.4 points out this tool. If you can't find the SIM removal tool, you can use any object with a similarly narrow end, such as a small paperclip or a safety pin.

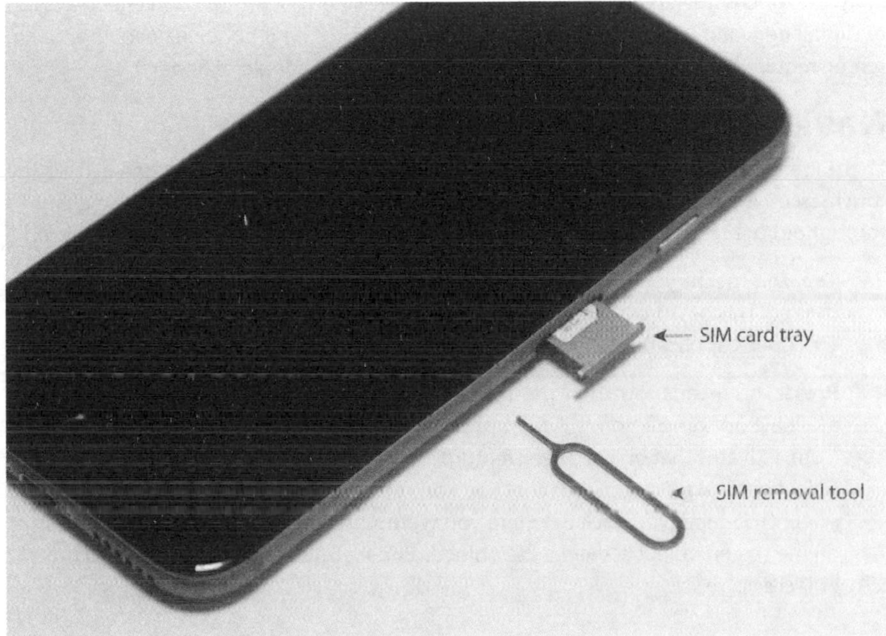

1.4 Push a SIM removal tool or pin into the hole to eject the tray.

2. **Push the SIM removal tool into the hole that appears on the SIM card tray.** This tray appears just below the Side button, as shown in Figure 1.4. Insert the tool until the tray ejects.

3. **Carefully lay the SIM card into the SIM card tray.** To ensure you insert the card correctly, match the notch in one corner of the SIM card with the corresponding notch in the tray.
4. **Reinsert the SIM card tray until you feel a soft click as the tray slides into its correct position.** Your SIM card is ready to use.

Operating the Touchscreen

The most distinctive feature of the iPhone is its versatile touchscreen. You can zoom in and out, scroll through lists, drag items here and there, and even type messages. Amazingly, the touchscreen requires no external hardware to do all this. You don't need a stylus or digital pen, and you don't need to attach anything to the iPhone. Instead, the touchscreen requires just your finger (or, for some operations, a couple of fingers).

Navigating the touchscreen

There are a few maneuvers that you need to be familiar with to successfully use the touchscreen in all its glory. Take some time to try these now. I'll refer to these gestures throughout the rest of the book, so play around and make sure you understand them:

- **Tap.** This means you use your finger to quickly press and release the screen where desired. This gesture is what you use to initiate just about any action on the iPhone. This opens applications, activates options, enters text boxes, and much more.
- **Press.** This means you apply pressure to the screen to activate the 3D Touch feature available on some iPhones. A light press on a screen object (such as a Home screen icon) activates that object's Peek feature, which either gives you a sneak peek of the object or displays commands that you can run on the object. If you then release the screen, iOS takes you back to where you were. Otherwise, a slightly harder press on the screen object activates the object's Pop feature, which takes you into the object's app.

Note

3D Touch is available on iPhone models 6s, 6s Plus, 7, 7 Plus, 8, 8 Plus, X, XS, and XS Max. iPhone models XR, SE (2nd edition), 11, 11 Pro, 11 Pro Max, 12, 12 mini, 12 Pro, and 12 Pro Max all replace 3D Touch with Haptic Touch, which recognizes a long press (that is, a press that lasts a few seconds) instead of actual screen pressure.

- **Double-tap.** This is what it sounds like: two quick taps with your finger. In applications such as Photos or Safari, it zooms in on images or chunked parts of web pages. A second double-tap zooms back out.
- **Swipe and flick.** To swipe means to drag your finger across the screen. You use this technique to scroll through lists, drag items to different spots, and unlock the iPhone. Flicking is just an exaggerated swipe. This rapidly scrolls through lists. Flick your finger up and down (or sometimes left and right) on the screen and the iPhone rapidly scrolls through the list. The faster the flick, the faster the scroll. Touch the screen to stop the scrolling process.
- **Spread and pinch.** You use these techniques to zoom in on or out of the screen. To spread means to move two fingers apart, and you use it to zoom in; to pinch means to move two fingers closer together, and you use it to zoom out. This is especially useful when viewing web pages because the text is often too small to read. Spread to zoom in on the text, making it readable, and pinch to return to the full screen for easy scrolling and navigation.

Searching your iPhone

Parkinson's Law of Data pithily encapsulates an inescapable fact of digital life: "Data expands to fill the space available for storage." With each new iteration of the iPhone, the space available for storage keeps getting larger: from 4GB in the original phone to 512GB in a top-of-the-line iPhone 12. So, following Parkinson's Law, we keep adding more data to our iPhones: music, photos, videos, email messages, Safari bookmarks, and on and on.

That's cool because it means you can bring more of your digital world with you wherever you go, but there's another law that quickly comes into play; call it The Law of Digital Needles in Electronic Haystacks: "The more data you have, the harder it is to find what you need." Fortunately, iOS rides to the rescue by adding welcome search features to the iPhone.

If you use a Mac, then you probably know how indispensable the Spotlight search feature is. It's just a humble text box, but Spotlight enables you to find *anything* on your Mac in just a blink or two of an eye. It's an essential tool in this era of massive hard drives. (Windows users get much the same functionality with taskbar searches.)

The size of your iPhone storage might pale in comparison to your desktop's drive, but you can still pack an amazing amount of stuff into that tiny package, so you really need a way to search your entire iPhone, including email, contacts, calendars, bookmarks, apps, and much more. And, best of all, Spotlight on the iPhone is just as easy to use as Spotlight on the Mac:

1. **Return to any Home screen.**

2. **Swipe right to navigate the Home screens until you can't go any farther.** You should now see a screen that includes a Search box at the top.

Genius

An often-quicker way to get to the Search box is to swipe down from the top-left corner to display the Notification Center and then swipe right.

3. **Tap in the Search box and then enter your search text.** Your iPhone immediately begins displaying items that match your text as you type, as shown in Figure 1.5.

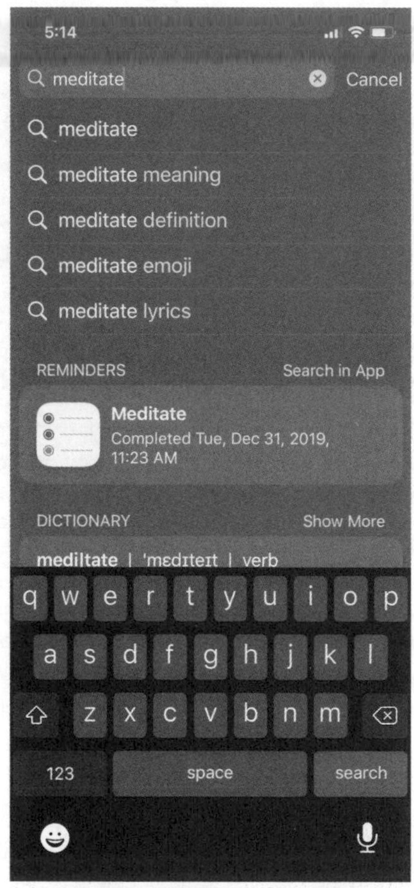

1.5 Flick down on the Home screen and then type your search text.

4. **Tap Search to see the complete results.** If you see the item you're looking for, tap it to open it.

Genius

Spotlight looks for a wide variety of items not only on your iPhone, but also on the Internet, iTunes, the App Store, and more. If you find you're getting too many results, you can configure Spotlight to not show results from certain apps. Tap Settings and then tap Siri & Search. In the Siri & Search screen, tap an app you want to remove from Search. Then tap the Show App in Search switch to Off and the Show Content in Search switch to Off.

Switching between running apps

Your iPhone is capable of *multitasking*, which enables you to run multiple apps at the same time. This is useful if, say, you're playing a game and an email message comes in. You can switch to the message, read it, respond to it, and then resume your game right where you left off.

So how do you switch from one app to another? It depends on your iPhone model:

- If your iPhone has a notch at the top of the screen (pointed out later in Figure 1.11), slide a finger up from the bottom edge of the screen and then pause about halfway up the screen.
- For all other iPhone models, double-press the Home button (that is, press the Home button twice in succession).

Either way, you end up at the multitasking screen, which displays thumbnail versions of your running apps. Flick left or right to bring the app thumbnail into view and then tap the app to switch to it.

Genius

To help you navigate the list of running apps, shut down any apps you won't be using for a while. Display the multitasking screen and then drag any app you want to shut down to the top of the screen.

Typing on the keyboard

You can type on your iPhone, although don't expect to pound out the prose as easily as you can on your computer. The on-screen keyboard (see Figure 1.6) is a bit too small for rapid and accurate typing, but once you get used to it (which doesn't take all that long), you'll be able to tap text fast enough to get the job done.

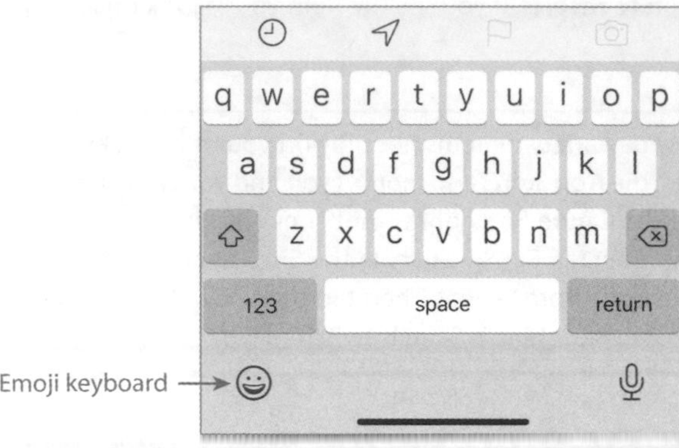

1.6 Trust the touchscreen even though the keys may be small.

To use the keyboard, tap into an area that requires text input, and the keyboard appears automatically. Tap the keys that you want to enter. As you touch each key, a magnified version of the letter pops up. If you touch the wrong key, slide your finger over to the correct one. The keyboard does not enter a key until your finger comes off the screen.

Genius

If you find yourself trying to type on your iPhone using one hand, you might find it hard to reach all the keys unless you have an exceptionally long thumb. To make things easier on yourself, tap and hold the Emoji keyboard icon (pointed out in Figure 1.6) and then choose either the Right keyboard (if you're right-handed) or the Left keyboard (if you're left-handed). These keyboards shift the keys right and left, respectively, for easier one-handed typing.

Using special keys

The keyboard has a few specialty keys that allow you to do some tricks:

- **Shift.** This key is a little upward-pointing arrow to the left of the Z key. Tap this key once to engage Shift. The letter keys change to uppercase, and the Shift key changes to a black arrow on a white background. The next letter you type will be a capital letter, at which point the Shift key returns to normal automatically (and the letter keys return to their lowercase versions).
- **123.** Tap this key to display the numeric keyboard, which includes numbers and most punctuation marks. The key then changes to ABC. Tap ABC to return to the standard keyboard.

- **#+=.** This key appears within the numeric keyboard. Tap this key to enter yet another keyboard that contains more punctuation marks as well as a few symbols that aren't used frequently.
- **Backspace.** This key is shaped like a left-pointing arrow with an X inside it, and it appears to the right of the M key. This key deletes at three different speeds:
  - The first speed deletes in response to a single tap, which deletes just a single letter.
  - The second speed deletes in response to being held. If you hold the delete key, it begins moving backward through letters and won't stop after a single letter.
  - The third speed kicks in if you hold the delete key long enough. This deletes entire words.
- **Return.** This key moves to the next line when you're typing text. However, this key often changes names and functions, depending on what you're doing. For example, you saw earlier (see Figure 1.5) that this becomes the Search key when you invoke the Search screen.

Editing text

Everyone asks me how you're supposed to move throughout the text to edit it. The only obvious option is to delete all the way back to your error, which is impractical to say the least. The solution is in the touchscreen, which enables you to zoom in on the specific section of text you want to edit. Follow these steps.

1. **Press and hold your finger on the line you want to edit.** iPhone displays the text inside a magnifying glass, and within that text you see the cursor (you might need to angle your iPhone just so to see the cursor).
2. **Slide your finger along the line.** As you slide, the cursor moves through the text in the same direction.
3. **When the cursor is where you want to begin editing, remove your finger.**

Understanding predictive typing

As you type, the iPhone often tries to predict which word you want to use, and it displays its suggestions in a bar that appears just above the keyboard. (In earlier versions, a single suggestion appears in a little bubble underneath the current word.) This is called *predictive typing*, and the suggestions you see depend on the context of your writing.

First, the suggestion feature shows up with misspelled words. iPhone selects the text that it thinks you misspelled and then offers suggested alternatives. You have three ways to handle these suggestions:

- To accept the highlighted suggestion, tap the spacebar or any punctuation.
- To use another suggestion, tap it.
- To keep your typing as is, tap the suggestion that appears in quotation marks.

Second, as you type, the iPhone guesses what the next word might be. For example, if you type *happy*, iPhone suggests (among others) "Birthday" for the next word. If any of the suggested words is the one you want, tap it to enter the suggestion.

Selecting and copying noneditable text

How you select and then either cut or copy text depends on whether that text is editable or noneditable.

The simplest case is noneditable text, such as you get on a web page. In that scenario, when the text you want to use is on the screen, tap and hold anywhere within the text. After a second or two, your iPhone selects the text and displays blue selection handles around it, as shown in Figure 1.7. If necessary, tap and drag the selection handles to select more or less of the text and then tap Copy.

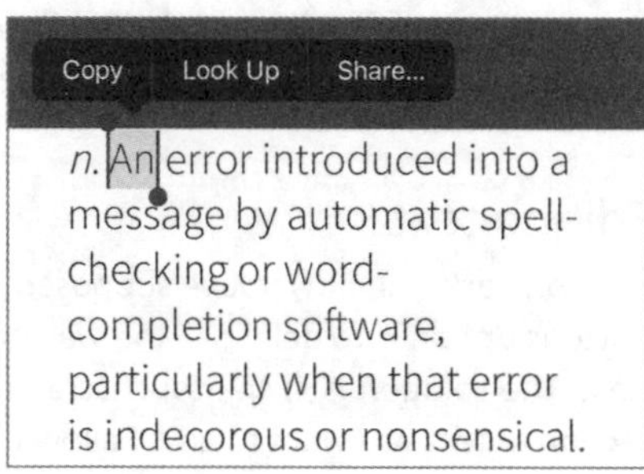

1.7 For text you can't edit, tap and hold within the text to select it and then tap Copy to copy it.

Selecting and then cutting or copying editable text

If the text is editable, such as the text in a note, an email message you're composing, or any text box, then the process is more involved, but only ever so slightly:

1. **Tap and hold anywhere within the text.** After a short pause for effect, your iPhone displays a couple of buttons above the text, as shown in Figure 1.8 (if you've previously copied some text, you'll also see a Paste button; more on this follows).
2. **Tap one of the following options:**
   - **Select.** Tap this button if you want to select only some of the text. Your iPhone displays blue selection handles around the word you tapped.

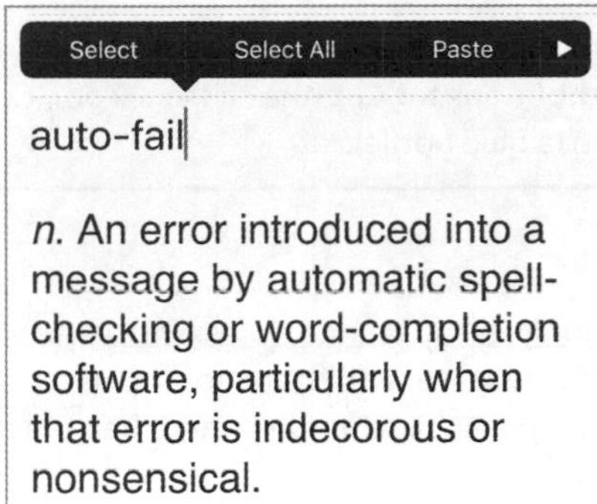

1.8 For editable text, tap and hold within the text to see these options.

- **Select All.** Tap this button if you prefer to select all the text. The iPhone displays the buttons shown in Figure 1.9; if you don't need to adjust the selection, skip to Step 4.

3. **Tap and drag the selection handles to select the text you want to work with.** The iPhone displays a new set of buttons above the text, as shown in Figure 1.9.

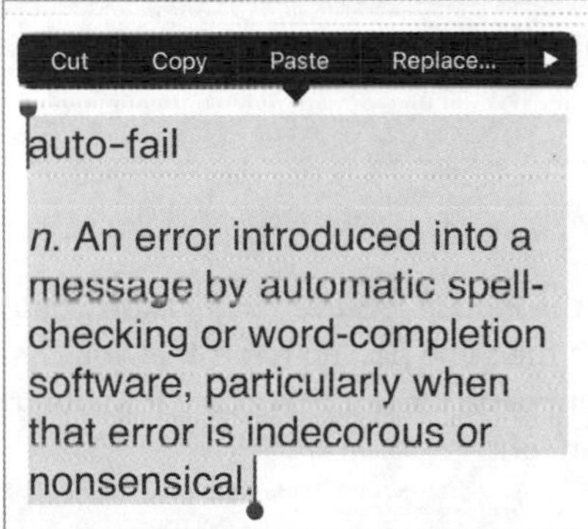

1.9 Select your text and then choose what you want to do with it.

4. **Tap the action you want iPhone to take with the text:**
   - **Cut.** Tap this button to remove the text and store it in the memory of your iPhone.
   - **Copy.** Tap this button to store a copy of the text in the memory of your iPhone.

Genius

On larger iPhones, rotate the phone into landscape mode to see an extended keyboard that includes dedicated buttons for Cut (the scissors icon), Copy (the letter A in a square), and Paste (a glue bottle).

Pasting text

With your text cut or copied and residing snugly in the memory of your iPhone, you're ready to paste the text. If you want to paste the text into a different app, open that app. Position the cursor where you want the text to appear, tap the cursor, and then tap Paste (see Figure 1.9). Your iPhone dutifully adds the cut or copied text.

Copying and pasting a photo

If you want to make a copy of a photo, such as an image shown on a web page, the process is more or less the same as copying noneditable text:

1. **Tap and hold the photo.** After a second or two, your iPhone displays a pop-up menu of image options.
2. **Tap Copy.** The iPhone copies the photo into its memory.
3. **Open the app where you want the copy of the photo to appear.**
4. **Position the cursor where you want the photo to appear and then tap the cursor.**
5. **Tap Paste.** The iPhone pastes the photo.

Undoing a paste

The Cut, Copy, and Paste commands make the iPhone feel even more like a computer. That's good, but it also means you can make the same pasting errors that you can with your regular computer. For example, you might paste the text or photo in the wrong spot, or once you've performed the paste, you might realize that you selected the wrong data.

Frustrating? Yes. A big problem? Nope! Slap your forehead lightly in exasperation and then perform one of the coolest iPhone tricks: Shake it. Your iPhone displays the options shown in Figure 1.10. Tap Undo Paste to reverse your most recent paste and then move on with your life.

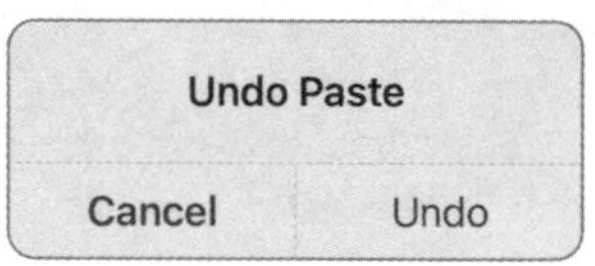

1.10 Reverse an imprudent paste by shaking the iPhone and then tapping Undo Paste.

Genius

On a larger iPhone, rotate into landscape mode and tap the Undo key (the semicircular arrow pointing to the left).

Running Your iPhone from the Control Center

As you read the rest of this book, you'll see that your iPhone is rightly called a "Swiss Army phone" because it's positively bristling with useful tools. However, unlike the easy-to-access tools in a typical Swiss Army knife, the tools on your iPhone aren't always so readily accessible. Most features and settings require several taps, which doesn't sound like much, but it can get old fast with features you use frequently.

Fortunately, iOS aims to solve that problem by offering the Control Center. This is a special screen that offers one-flick access to more than a dozen of the most useful features on your iPhone. By "one-flick access" I mean just this:

- If your iPhone has a notch at the top, flick down from the top-right edge of the screen (as pointed out in Figure 1.11).
- For all other iPhones, flick your finger up from the bottom of the screen.

This displays the Control Center, as shown in Figure 1.11, which also points out what each icon and control represents. (Depending on your iPhone model and the version of iOS it's running, you might see more or fewer icons than shown here.) Most of these features are covered elsewhere in the book, so I won't go into the details here. To hide the Control Center, tap any empty section of the Control Center screen.

Genius

You can customize the bottom row of the Control Center. Open the Settings app, tap Control Center, then add the controls you want and remove those you don't use.

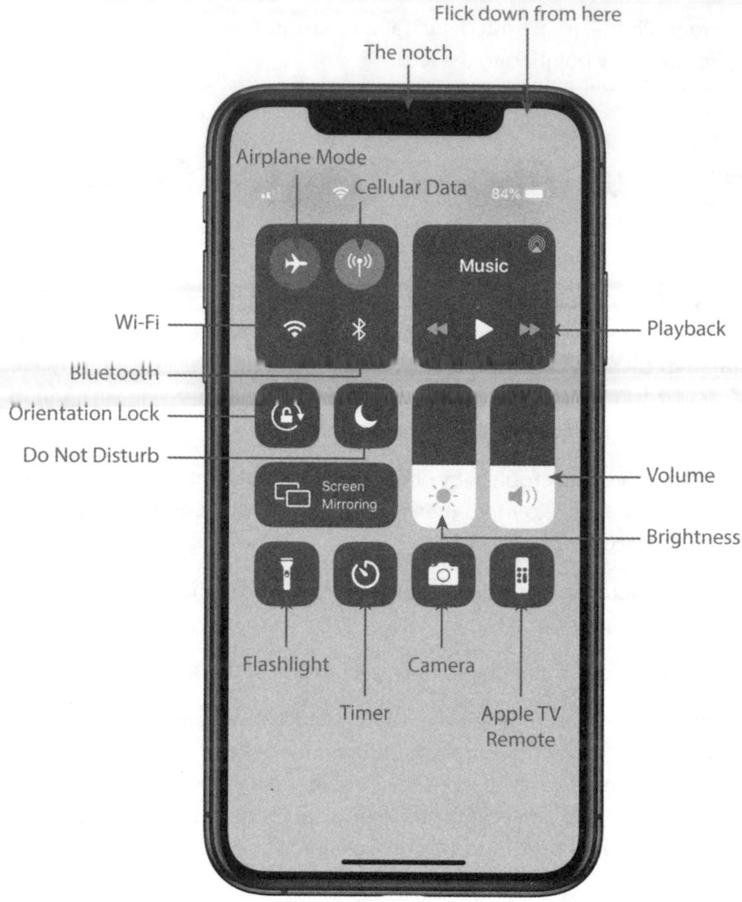

1.11 The Control Center offers "one-flick" access to some key iPhone features.

How Do I Configure My iPhone?

The iPhone is justly famous for its stylish design and its effortless touchscreen. However, although good looks and ease of use are important for any smartphone, it's what you do with that phone that's important. The iPhone helps by offering a lot of features, but chances are those features aren't set up to suit the way you work. Maybe your most-used Home screen icons aren't at the top of the screen where they should be, or perhaps your iPhone goes to sleep too soon. This chapter shows you how to configure your iPhone to solve these and many other annoyances so the phone works the way you do.

Customizing the Home Screen

The Home screen is your starting point for all things iPhone, and what could be simpler? Just tap an icon and the app launches right away. However, you can make the Home screen even more efficient by moving your four most-used icons to the iPhone Dock (the bottom section of each Home screen) and by moving your other often-used icons to the top row or left column of the main Home screen. You can do all this by rearranging the Home screen icons as follows:

1. **Display the Home screen.**
2. **Tap and hold any Home screen icon.** iOS displays a list of actions you can perform.
3. **Tap Edit Home Screen.** iOS starts the Home screen icons a wiggling.
4. **Tap and drag the icons into the positions you prefer.** To move an icon to a previous screen, tap and drag it to the left edge of the current screen. To move it to a later screen, tap and drag it to the right edge of the current screen. Next, wait for the new screen to appear and then drop the icon where you want it.
5. **Rearrange the existing Dock icons by dragging them left or right to change the order.**
6. **To replace a Dock icon, first tap and drag the icon off the Dock to create some space.** Then tap and drag any Home screen icon into the Dock.
7. **Stop the Home screen editing:**
   - If your iPhone has a notch at the top of the screen, tap Done, which appears to the right of the notch.
   - For all other iPhones, press the Home button.

   Your iPhone saves the new icon arrangement.

Creating an app folder

You can reduce the number of icons on the Home screens by taking advantage of a great feature called *app folders*. Just like a folder on your hard drive that can store multiple files, an app folder can store multiple app icons. This enables you to group related apps under a single icon, which not only reduces your overall Home screen clutter but can also make individual apps easier to find. Here are the steps to follow to create and populate an app folder:

1. **Navigate to the Home screen that contains at least one of the apps you want to include in your folder.**

2. **Tap and hold any Home screen icon.** iOS displays a list of actions you can perform.
3. **Tap Edit Home Screen.** The Home screen start wiggling.
4. **Tap and drag an icon that you want to include in the folder and drop it on another icon that you want to include in the same folder.** iOS creates the folder.
5. **Tap the folder.** iOS displays a text box so that you can name the folder, as shown in Figure 2.1.
6. **Tap inside the text box to edit the name and then tap Done when you finish.**
7. **Stop the Home screen editing:**
   - If your iPhone has a notch at the top of the screen, tap Done, which appears to the right of the notch.
   - For all other iPhones, press the Home button.

   Your iPhone saves your new icon arrangement.

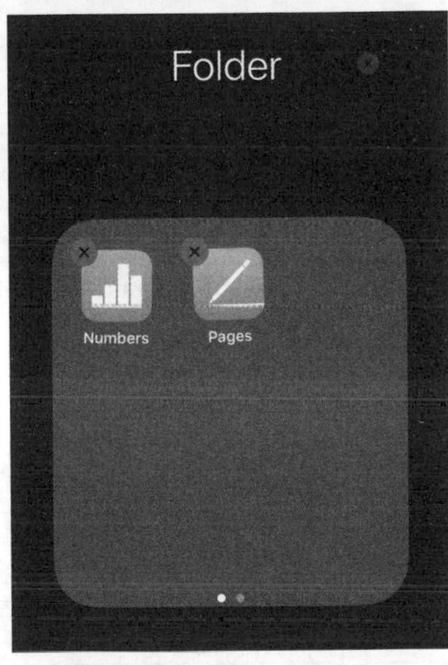

2.1 Drop one app icon on another to create an app folder.

To launch an app, tap the folder to open it and tap the app. To work with your app folders,
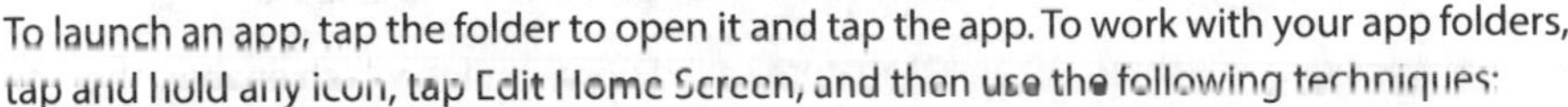
tap and hold any icon, tap Edit Home Screen, and then use the following techniques:

- **Add another app to a folder.** Tap and drag the app icon and drop it on the folder.
- **Rename a folder.** Tap the folder to open it and then edit the folder name.
- **Rearrange the apps within a folder.** Tap the folder to open it and then drag and drop the apps within the folder.
- **Remove an app from a folder.** Tap the folder to open it and then drag the app icon out of the folder.

Adding a web page bookmark to the Home screen

Do you have a web page that you visit all the time? If so, you can set up that page as a bookmark in the iPhone Safari browser, but there's an even faster way to access it: You can add it to the Home screen. Follow these steps to save a page as an icon on the Home screen:

1. **Use the Safari browser on your iPhone to navigate to the page you want to save.**
2. **Tap the Share icon (the arrow) at the bottom of the screen.** iPhone displays a list of actions.
3. **Tap Add to Home Screen.** iPhone prompts you to edit the web clip name.
4. **Edit the name as needed.**
5. **Tap Add.** iPhone adds the web clip to the Home screen and displays the Home screen.

Genius

If you make a bit of a mess of your Home screen or if someone else is going to be using your iPhone, you can reset the Home screen icons to their default layout. I tell you how this is done in Chapter 11.

Working with App Notifications

A lot of apps take advantage of an iOS feature called *notifications,* which enables them to send messages and other data to your iPhone. For example, the Facebook app displays an alert on your iPhone when a friend sends you a message. If an app supports notifications, then the first time you start it, your iPhone usually displays a message like the one shown in Figure 2.2, asking if you want to allow notifications for the app. Tap Allow if you're cool with that; if you're not, tap Don't Allow.

"Flickr" Would Like to Send You Notifications
Notifications may include alerts, sounds, and icon badges. These can be configured in Settings.
Don't Allow | Allow

2.2 Your iPhone lets you allow or disallow notifications for an app.

There are actually four kinds of notifications:

- **Sound.** This is a sound effect that plays when some app-related event occurs.

- **Alert.** This is a message that pops up on your iPhone screen. You must then tap a button to dismiss the message before you can continue working with your current app.
- **Banner.** This is a message that appears at the top of the screen. Unlike an alert, a banner allows you to keep using your current app and disappears automatically after a few seconds. If you prefer to switch to the app to view the message, tap the banner.
- **Badge.** This is a small, red icon that appears in the upper-right corner of an app icon. The icon usually displays a number, which might be the number of messages you have waiting for you on the server.

Displaying the Notification Center

If you miss an alert or banner or if you see a banner but ignore it, you can still eyeball your recent notification messages by displaying the Notification Center. This is a feature that combines all your recent alerts and banners in one handy location. So, not only can you see the most recent alert, but you can also see the last few so you don't miss anything.

Even better, displaying the Notification Center is a snap: Just swipe down from the top of the screen. The Notification Center displays your recent messages sorted by app. From here, you can either tap an item to switch to that app or swipe up from the bottom of the screen to hide the Notification Center.

Handling notifications within the Notification Center

Tapping a notification opens the associated app so that you can work with the item. For example, if the notification concerns a recently received email message, you might want to tap the notification to open Mail and read or delete the message. However, for simple actions (such as viewing an email), opening the app feels like overkill. Fortunately, the Notification Center can save you a tap or two by enabling you to handle notifications directly within the Notification Center:

- **View a notification.** Either tap and hold the notification or swipe left on the notification and then tap View. Note, too, that you often get more buttons that you can tap to handle the notification. For example, if you view an email message, you see two buttons: Mark as Read and Trash (see Figure 2.3).

2.3 View a notification to reveal one or more buttons that enable you to handle the item from within the Notification Center.

- **Manage an app's notifications.** Swipe left on a notification and then tap Manage. This brings up the following actions:
  - **Deliver Quietly.** Configures the app to deliver notifications without playing a sound or displaying a banner or badge.
  - **Turn Off.** Stops all notifications from the app.
  - **Settings.** Takes you to the app's notification settings, which I describe in the next section.
- **Clear one or more notifications.** Swipe left on the notification and then tap Clear. If the notifications are organized as a group in Notification Center, swipe left on the group and then tap Clear All.

Customizing notifications

For each app, your iPhone lets you toggle individual notification types (sounds, alerts, and badges), switch between banner and alert messages, or remove an app from the Notification Center altogether. You can also configure app notifications to appear in the Lock screen (with the Lock screen displayed, swipe down from the top of the screen to see the Notification Center). This is handy because you can see your notifications without having to unlock your iPhone.

Here's how to configure app notifications:

1. **On the Home screen, tap Settings.** The Settings app appears.
2. **Tap Notifications.** The Notifications screen appears.
3. **Tap the app you want to customize.** The app notification settings appear. Figure 2.4 shows the settings for the Reminders app. Note that not all apps support all possible settings.

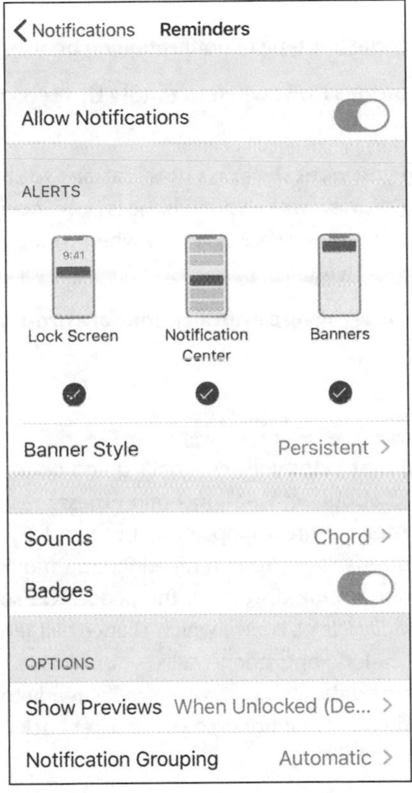

2.4 Use each app's notification settings to control notifications on your iPhone.

4. **If you prefer not to receive notifications from the app, tap the Allow Notifications switch to Off and then skip the rest of these steps.**
5. **In the Alerts section, tap the styles you prefer for message notifications.** Tap to toggle Lock Screen, Notification Center, or Banners.
6. **Tap Banner Style and then select the banner type you prefer for the app.** Tap Temporary to have each banner disappear automatically after a few seconds; tap Persistent to have each banner stay on-screen until you dismiss it.
7. **If the app supports sound notifications, you'll see one of the following setting types:**
   - **Sounds menu.** Tap this to select a sound to play or tap None to play no sound.
   - **Sounds switch.** Tap this switch to toggle this type of notification on or off.
8. **If the app supports badges, use the Badges Icon switch to toggle this type of notification on or off.**
9. **Tap Show Previews and choose when you want the app's notifications to show a preview.** Always means you can see a preview when your iPhone is both locked and unlocked, When Unlocked means you can see a preview only when your phone isn't locked, and Never disables the preview feature.
10. **Tap Notification Grouping to choose how the app's notifications are grouped in the Notification Center.**

Configuring Do Not Disturb settings

The Notification Center is a truly useful tool that helps you see what's going on in your world at a glance and gives you a heads-up about activities, incoming messages, app happenings, and more. The Notification Center is a great innovation, but it's also a distracting one with its banners, alerts, and sounds. If you're in a meeting, at a movie, or going to sleep, you certainly don't want your iPhone disturbing the peace. iOS solves this conundrum by offering a feature called Do Not Disturb, which silences all iPhone distractions — including Notification Center alerts and phone calls — but keeps your iPhone online so that it can continue to receive data. That way, when you're ready to get back to the action, all your new data is already on your iPhone, so you can get back up to speed quickly.

You can get even more out of Do Not Disturb by configuring it to suit the way you work. Here are the steps to follow:

1. **Tap Settings to open the Settings app.**
2. **Tap Do Not Disturb.** The Do Not Disturb screen appears.

3. **To set a time to automatically activate and deactivate Do Not Disturb, tap the Scheduled switch to On.** You then use the From controls to set the start time and use the To controls to set the end time.
4. **If you want Do Not Disturb to handle calls and notifications normally (that is, nonsilently) when your iPhone is unlocked, tap the Only While iPhone Is Locked option.**
5. **If you want to allow certain calls even when Do Not Disturb is activated, tap Allow Calls From and then tap who you want to get through: Everyone, No One, Favorites (that is, anyone in the Phone app's Favorites list), or a particular contact group.**
6. **If you want Do Not Disturb to allow a call through when the same person calls twice within 3 minutes, leave the Repeated Calls switch in the On position.** If you don't want to allow this exception, tap the Repeated Calls switch to Off.

Note

To turn on Do Not Disturb outside of the scheduled time, tap Settings, tap Do Not Disturb, and then tap the Do Not Disturb switch to On. Alternatively, open the Control Center and tap Do Not Disturb (pointed out in Figure 1.11).

Genius

Do Not Disturb is perfect for when you're driving because if there was ever a time your iPhone shouldn't disturb you, it's when you're behind the wheel. To make sure this works, tap Activate in the Do Not Disturb While Driving section and then tap Automatically (which means iOS activates Do Not Disturb when it detects that your car is moving). If your iPhone connects to Bluetooth in the car, you could alternatively tap the When Connected to Car Bluetooth option.

More Useful iPhone Configuration Techniques

You've seen quite a few handy iPhone customization tricks so far, but you're not done yet — not by a long shot. The next few sections take you through a few more heartwarmingly useful iPhone customization techniques.

Changing the name of your iPhone

Feel free to rename your iPhone for the sake of giving it a cool or snappy name if the mood strikes. Here's how:

1. **On the iPhone Home screen, tap Settings.** The Settings screen appears.
2. **Tap General.** The General settings appear.
3. **Tap About.** The About page appears.
4. **Tap Name.** The Settings app displays a text box with the current name of your iPhone.
5. **Edit the name as you see fit.**

Turning sounds on and off

Your iPhone is often a noisy little thing that makes all manner of rings, beeps, and boops, seemingly at the slightest provocation. None of this may bother you when you're on your own, but if you're in a meeting, at a movie, or anywhere else where extraneous sounds are unwelcome, you might want to turn off some (or all) of the iPhone sound effects. You can control exactly which sounds your iPhone utters by following these steps:

1. **On the Home screen, tap Settings.** The Settings app appears.
2. **Tap Sounds & Haptics.** The Sounds & Haptics screen appears.
3. **The two switches in the Vibrate section determine whether your iPhone vibrates when the phone rings or is in Silent Mode.** Vibrating probably isn't all that important in Ring Mode, so feel free to change this setting to Off. The exception is if you reduce and/or lock the ringer volume (see Steps 4 and 5), in which case setting Vibrate on Ring to On might help you notice an incoming call. Vibrating in Silent Mode is a good idea, so On is a good choice for the Vibrate on Silent setting.
4. **In the Ringer and Alerts section, drag the volume slider to set the volume of the ringtone that plays when a call comes in.**
5. **To lock the ringer volume, tap the Change with Buttons switch to Off.** This means that pressing the volume buttons on the side of the iPhone will have no effect on the ringer volume.

Genius

Locking the ringer volume is a good idea because it prevents one of the major iPhone frustrations: missing a call because the ringer volume has been muted accidentally (for example, by your iPhone getting jostled in a purse or pocket).

6. **To set a different default ringtone, tap Ringtone to open the Ringtone screen.** Tap the ringtone you want to use (iPhone plays a preview) and then tap Back to return to the Sounds screen.
7. **For each of the other events in the list (from Text Tone to AirDrop), tap the event and then tap the sound you want to hear.** You can also tap None to turn off the event sound.
8. **To turn off the sound that your iPhone makes each time you tap a key on the virtual keyboard, tap the Keyboard Clicks switch to Off.**
9. **To turn off the sound that your iPhone makes when you lock and unlock it, tap the Lock Sound switch to Off.**

Genius

One of the truly annoying iPhone sound effects is the clicking sound made by each key when using the on-screen keyboard. If it doesn't make you batty after 5 minutes, it will certainly drive anyone within earshot to thoughts of violence. So, I strongly recommend tapping the Keyboard Clicks setting to Off. There, that's better.

Customizing the keyboard

Did you know that the keyboard changes depending on the app you use? For example, the regular keyboard features a spacebar at the bottom. However, if you're entering an email address in the Mail app, the keyboard that appears offers a smaller spacebar and uses the extra space to show an at sign (@) key and a period (.) key, two characters that are part of any email address. Nice! Here are some other nice innovations you get with the iPhone keyboard:

- **Auto-Capitalization.** If you type a punctuation mark that indicates the end of a sentence — for example, a period (.), a question mark (?), or an exclamation mark (!) — or if you press Return to start a new paragraph, the iPhone automatically activates the Shift key, because it assumes you're starting a new sentence.

- **Double-tapping the spacebar.** This activates a keyboard shortcut: Instead of entering two spaces, the iPhone automatically enters a period (.) followed by a space. This is a welcome bit of efficiency because otherwise you'd have to tap the Number key (123) to display the numbers and punctuation marks, tap the period (.), and then tap the spacebar.

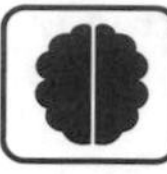

Genius

Typing a number or punctuation mark normally requires three taps: tapping Number (123), tapping the number or symbol, and then tapping ABC. Here's a faster way: Use one finger to tap and hold the Number key to open the numeric keyboard, use a second finger to tap the number or punctuation symbol you want, and then release the Number key. This types the number or symbol and returns you to the regular keyboard.

- **Auto-Correction.** For many people, one of the keys to quick iPhone typing is to clear the mind and just tap away without worrying about accuracy. In many cases, you'll actually be rather amazed at how accurate this willy-nilly approach can be. Why does it work? The secret is the Auto-Correction feature on your iPhone, which eyeballs what you're typing and automatically corrects any errors. For example, if you tap *hte,* your iPhone automatically corrects this to *the*. Your iPhone displays the suggested correction before you complete the word (say, by tapping a space or a comma), and you can reject the suggestion by tapping the typed text that appears with quotation marks in the predictive typing bar. If you find you never use the predictive suggestions, you can turn them off to save a bit of screen real estate.
- **Caps Lock.** One thing the iPhone keyboard doesn't seem to have is a Caps Lock feature that, when activated, enables you to type all-uppercase letters. To do this, you need to tap and hold the Shift key and then use a different finger to tap the uppercase letters. However, the iPhone actually does have a Caps Lock feature: Double-tap Shift to turn Caps Lock on (which is indicated on the Shift key with a horizontal bar under the arrow), then tap Shift to turn Caps Lock off.
- **Slide to Type.** If you're *really* in a hurry, you might resent the split second that elapses between the tap of each key. To shave even that small amount of time off your typing chores, you can use the Slide to Type feature, where instead of tapping each key individually, you quickly slide your finger from one letter to the next, only lifting your finger when you complete each word. (Yep, iOS adds a space automatically.) It takes a bit of getting used to, but it can make entering text crazy-fast.
- **Character preview.** This feature displays a pop-up version of each character as you tap it. This is great for iPhone keyboard rookies because it helps them be sure

they're typing accurately, but veterans often find it distracting. Some even complain that it's a security risk because the letters pop up even when you're typing a password! That might be why Apple chooses to turn off character preview by default, but you can turn it on if you miss it.

To change the settings for any of these keyboard features, follow these steps:

1. **On the Home screen, tap Settings.** The Settings app appears.
2. **Tap General.** The General screen appears.
3. **Tap Keyboard.** The Keyboard screen appears.
4. **Use the switches — including Auto-Capitalization, Auto-Correction, Enable Caps Lock, Predictive, Slide to Type, Character Preview, and "." Shortcut — to toggle keyboard features off and on as you prefer.**

Setting up Apple Pay

Prior to 2020, paying for things by waving your phone at a contactless reader was convenient, but not essential. Then the Great Pandemic of 2020 came along, and suddenly the virtues of going "contactless" became glaringly obvious. If you'd like to use your iPhone to pay for stuff without having to press any buttons or insert a payment card, then you need to configure Apply Pay on your device. Here's what you do:

1. **Open the Settings app.**
2. **Tap Wallet & Apple Pay.** The Wallet & Apple Pay screen appears.
3. **Tap Add Card.**
4. **Tap Continue.** iOS displays a camera frame.
5. **Place your payment card on a flat surface and then position the camera frame so that the card fills the frame.** You might have to hover the frame over the card for a few seconds before iOS recognizes it and displays the Card Details screen.
6. **Double-check that your name and card number are accurate; then tap Next.** If either or both your name and card number contain an error, edit as needed and then tap Next.
7. **Select the card's expiration month and year (if needed; these should already be entered for you), type the card's three-digit security code, and then tap Next.** iOS displays some terms and conditions.
8. **Read the terms and conditions (I jest, of course) and then tap Agree.**

9. **If your card requires verification, tap the method you prefer to use (such as Text Message), tap Next, and then enter the verification code when you receive it.** Note that if your verification device is the same iPhone as the one you're using, iOS will enter the verification code for you automatically.
10. **The next steps depend on whether you're adding your first card or a subsequent card:**
    - **You're adding your first payment card.** iOS adds the payment card to your iPhone's digital wallet and then shows a screen with instructions on using Apple Pay. Tap Continue. iOS returns you to the Wallet & Apple Pay screen.
    - **You're adding a subsequent payment card.** iOS asks if you want this new card to be the default for payments. If so, tap Use as Default Card; otherwise, tap Not Now. iOS adds the payment card to your iPhone's digital wallet and then returns you to the Wallet & Apple Pay screen.
11. **If you want to add more payment cards, repeat Steps 3 through 10.**

You might be wondering how you pay for something when you have multiple payment cards. Here's how:

- To pay with the default card, double-press either the Side button (if your iPhone has Face ID) or the Home button, verify that it's you (with Face ID, Touch ID, or a passcode), and then hold the phone near the contactless reader until the transaction is complete.
- To pay with another card, double-press either the Side button (if your iPhone has Face ID) or the Home button and then verify that it's you (with Face ID, Touch ID, or a passcode). You now see a screen similar to the one shown in Figure 2.5, which shows your default card at the top and your other cards at the bottom. Tap the bottom cards, tap the card you want to use, and then hold the phone near the contactless reader until the transaction is complete.

Note

Face ID obviously won't work if you're wearing a mask! In that case, iOS enables you to use a secondary verification method, such as your passcode.

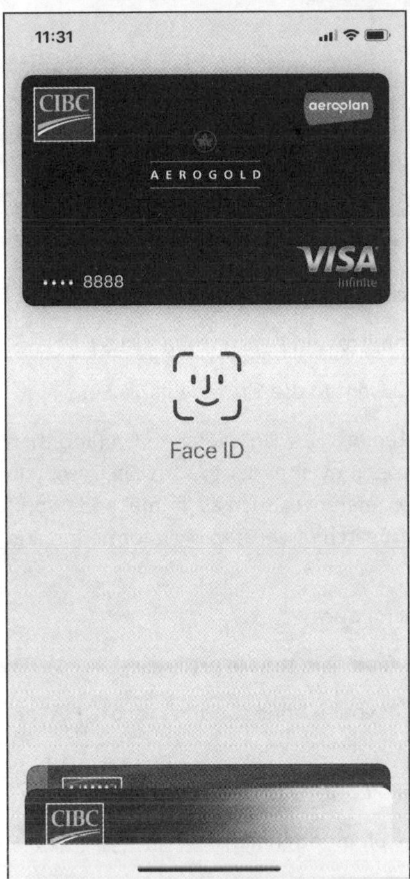

2.5 The wallet shows your default card at the top and your other cards at the bottom.

Genius

To specify a different payment card as the default, follow Steps 1 and 2 to open the Wallet & Apple Pay screen, tap Default Card, and then tap the card you prefer to use as the default. Alternatively, open the Wallet app and then tap and drag the card you want to use as the default to the front of the stack.

Configuring Siri

You can make things happen on your iPhone via voice commands by using the Siri app, which not only lets you launch apps, but also gives you voice control over web searching, appointments, contacts, reminders, map navigation, text messages, notes, and much more.

First, make sure that Siri is activated by tapping Settings on the Home screen, tapping Siri & Search, and then doing one of the following:

- If your iPhone supports Face ID, tap the Press Side Button for Siri switch to On.
- For all other iPhone models, tap the Press Home for Siri switch to On.

Either way, when iOS asks you to confirm that you want to use Siri, tap Enable Siri.

While you're here, you might want to tap the Listen for "Hey Siri" switch to On (and then run through a brief setup procedure), which makes it even easier to start Siri. Also, you should tell Siri who you are so that when you use references such as "home" and "work," Siri knows what you're talking about. On the Siri & Search screen, tap My Information and then tap your item in the Contacts list.

You crank up Siri by using any of the following techniques:

- Saying "Hey Siri" (assuming you enabled this feature in the Siri settings).
- Pressing and holding either the Side button (if your iPhone supports Face ID) or the Home button.
- Pressing and holding the Mic button on your iPhone headphones.
- Pressing and holding the Mic equivalent on a Bluetooth headset.

Siri is often easier to use if you define relationships within it. So, for example, instead of saying "Call Sandy Evans," you can simply say "Call mom." You can define relationships in two ways:

- **Within the Contacts app.** Open the Contacts app, tap your contact item, tap Edit, tap Add Related Name, and then tap the relationship you want to use. Tap the blue More icon to open the All Contacts list and then tap the person you want to add to the field.
- **Within Siri.** Say "*Name* is my *relationship*," where *Name* is the person's name as given in your Contacts list, and *relationship* is the connection, such as *wife, husband, spouse, partner, brother, sister, mother,* or *father*. When Siri asks you to confirm, say "Yes."

Controlling your privacy

Third-party apps occasionally request permission to use the data from another app. For example, an app might need access to your contacts, your calendars, your photos, or your Twitter and Facebook accounts. You can always deny these requests, of course, but if you've allowed access to an app in the past, you might later change your mind and decide you'd prefer to revoke that access. Fortunately, iOS offers a Privacy feature that enables you to control which apps have access to your data. Here's how it works:

1. **On the Home screen, tap Settings to open the Settings app.**
2. **Tap Privacy.** The Privacy screen appears.
3. **Tap the app or feature for which you want to control access.** Your iPhone displays a list of third-party apps that have requested access to the app or feature.
4. **To revoke a third-party app's access to the app or feature, tap its switch to Off.**

Protecting Your iPhone

These days, an iPhone is much more than just a phone. You use it to surf the web, send and receive email and text messages, manage your contacts and schedules, find your way in the world, and much more. This is handy, for sure, but it also means that your iPhone is jammed with tons of information about you. Even though you might not store the nuclear launch codes on your iPhone, chances are what is on it is pretty important to you. Therefore, you should take steps to protect your iPhone, and that's what the next few sections are all about.

Locking your iPhone with a passcode

If you have sensitive or confidential information on your phone or if you want to avoid digital joyrides that run up massive roaming or data charges, you need to lock your iPhone. You do that by specifying a passcode that must be entered before anyone can use the iPhone. The default in iOS is a six-digit passcode, but you can change that either to a simple four-digit passcode or to a custom code that is longer and more complex and uses any combination of numbers, letters, and symbols. Follow these steps to set up your passcode:

1. **On the Home screen, tap Settings.** The Settings app appears.
2. **Tap Face ID & Passcode.** If your iPhone supports Touch ID, tap Touch ID & Passcode instead.

3. **Tap Turn Passcode On.** The Set Passcode screen appears.
4. **If you prefer to use something other than a six-digit passcode, tap Passcode Options and then tap the type of passcode you want to use.**
5. **Tap your passcode.** For security, the characters appear in the passcode box as dots.
6. **If you're entering a custom passcode, tap Next.** Your iPhone prompts you to reenter the passcode.
7. **Tap your passcode again.**
8. **If you're entering a custom passcode, tap Done.**

Caution

You really, really need to remember your iPhone passcode. If you forget it, you're locked out of your own phone. The only way to get back in is to restore the data and settings to your iPhone from an existing backup (as described in Chapter 11).

Caution

Auto-Lock is a crucial feature if you've protected your iPhone with a passcode lock because if your iPhone never sleeps, it never locks, either. To make sure your iPhone sleeps automatically, open the Settings app, tap Display & Brightness, tap Auto-Lock, and then tap the interval you want to use.

Unlocking your iPhone biometrically

Protecting your iPhone with a passcode is just good sense in this age of so-called "iCrime," where thieves routinely go "Apple picking" by snatching iPhones and other Apple devices from the unwary. With a passcode acting as a digital barrier between the crook and your iPhone, at least your personal data is safe from prying eyes. Yes, a passcode is a smart safety precaution, but it's not always a convenient one. Having to tap that four-character (or more) code many times during the day adds a small but nevertheless unwelcome annoyance to using the iPhone.

As an extra (and more convenient) layer of security, you can configure your iPhone with a biometric lock, which means you can only unlock the device using either your face or a fingerprint:

- If your iPhone supports Face ID, open the Settings app, tap Face ID & Passcode, tap Set Up Face ID, and then follow the instructions.

- If your iPhone supports Touch ID, open the Settings app, tap Touch ID & Passcode, tap Set Up Face ID, and then follow the instructions. Note that you can set up multiple fingerprints for Touch ID.

Configuring parental controls

If your children have access to your iPhone or if they have iPhones of their own, then you might be a bit worried about some of the content they might be exposed to on the web, on YouTube, or in other apps. Similarly, you might not want them installing apps or giving away their current location.

For all those and similar parental worries, you can sleep better at night by activating the Screen Time app's parental controls on your iPhone. These controls restrict the content and activities that kids can see and do. Here's how to set them up:

1. **On the Home screen, tap Settings.** The Settings app appears.
2. **Tap Screen Time.** The Screen Time settings appear.
3. **Tap Turn On Screen Time and then tap Continue.** iOS asks if you're configuring Screen Time for yourself or for a child.
4. **Tap This is My Child's iPhone.** The Downtime screen appears.
5. **Set the start and end times for when your child is not allowed to use the phone without your permission and then tap Set Downtime.** The App Limits screen appears.
6. **Select each of the app categories you want to limit (or, select All Apps and Categories to cover everything), tap Set, select the maximum amount of time your child is allowed for the selected categories, and then tap Set App Limit.** The Content & Privacy screen appears.
7. **Tap Continue.** iOS prompts you to enter a Screen Time passcode.
8. **Tap a passcode (twice).** iOS asks for an Apple ID to use to recover your Screen Time passcode.
9. **Type your Apple ID email and password and then tap OK.**

Locating and protecting a lost iPhone

If there's a downside to using a smartphone (particularly one as smart as the iPhone), it's that you end up with a pretty large chunk of your life on that phone. Initially, that may sound like a good thing, but if you happen to lose your phone, you've also lost that chunk of your life. Plus, assuming you haven't configured your iPhone with a passcode lock, as described earlier, you've opened a gaping privacy hole because anyone can now delve into your data. I'm sure you'd love to find your iPhone because it's expensive and there's just something creepy about the thought of some stranger flicking through your stuff.

You can locate a lost iPhone using an app called Find My. (You can also use this feature through your iCloud account, if you have one.) Find My uses the GPS sensor embedded inside your iPhone to locate the device. You can also use Find My to play a sound on your iPhone, remotely lock it and send a message, or, in a real pinch, remotely delete your data. The next few sections provide the details.

Note

You might think that a fatal flaw with Find My iPhone is that someone who has your iPhone can easily turn off the feature and disable it. Fortunately, that's not the case because your iPhone comes with a feature called Activation Lock, which means that a person can turn off Find My iPhone only by entering your Apple ID password.

Activating Find My iPhone

Find My works by looking for a particular signal that your iPhone beams out into the ether. This signal is turned off by default, so you need to turn it on if you ever plan to use Find My. Here are the steps to follow:

1. **Add your iCloud account, if you haven't done so already, as described in Chapter 10.** When you add the account, be sure to tap OK when iCloud asks if it can use your location.
2. **On the Home screen, tap Settings.** The Settings app appears.
3. **Tap your name at the top of the Settings screen.** Your Apple ID settings appear.
4. **Tap Find My.** The Find My screen appears.
5. **Tap Find My iPhone and then tap the Find My iPhone switch to On.**

Genius

Your lost iPhone might just be somewhere no one can find it. In that case, the danger is that the iPhone battery will die before you have a chance to locate it using Find My. To make this less likely, be sure to activate the Send Last Location switch. This configures your iPhone to send you the phone's last known location as soon as it detects that its battery is nearly done.

With Find My iPhone now active on your iPhone, you can use the Find My app or iCloud to locate it at any time. The next two sections show you how to do this.

Locating your iPhone using the Find My app

Follow these steps to see your lost iPhone on a map using the Find My app:

1. **On an iPhone, iPad, or iPod touch that has the Find My app installed, tap the app to launch it.**
2. **Tap Devices.** Find My displays a list of devices.
3. **Tap your lost iPhone.** The Find My app locates the iPhone on a map.

Locating your iPhone using iCloud

Follow these steps to see your lost iPhone on a map using iCloud:

1. **Log in to your iCloud account.**
2. **Click Find iPhone and, if prompted, enter your iCloud password.** The iCloud Find My iPhone application appears.
3. **Click All Devices.** iCloud displays a list of your devices.
4. **Click your iPhone in the list.** iCloud locates your iPhone on a map.

Getting an email message when your iPhone comes online

Find My iPhone is useful only if you can, you know, *find* your iPhone. That won't happen if your iPhone is powered off or not connected to the Internet. You could keep refreshing the list of devices, but it could be hours before your iPhone comes online. To avoid a constant vigil, you can tell Find My to send an email message to your iCloud account as soon as your iPhone comes online:

1. **Display the My Devices list.**
2. **Tap or click your iPhone in the devices list.** Find My displays information about your iPhone.
3. **If Find My iPhone has no location data for your iPhone, select Notify When Found.**

Playing a sound on your iPhone

If you misplace your phone, the first thing you should try is calling your number using another phone so you can (hopefully!) hear it ringing. That might not work, however, because your phone might have Ring/Silent switched to Silent Mode, it might be in Airplane Mode, or you might not have another phone handy. In any case, you only get so many rings before the call goes to voicemail, so unless you locate your phone right away, calling your number isn't always the best solution.

Your next step when looking for a lost iPhone is to use Find My to play a sound on your phone. This sound plays even if your iPhone is in Silent Mode or Airplane Mode, and it plays loudly even if your iPhone has its volume turned down or muted. Here's how it works:

1. **Display the My Devices list.**
2. **Tap or click your iPhone in the list.** Find My locates your iPhone on a map.
3. **Tap or click Play Sound.** Find My iPhone begins playing the sound on your iPhone, and it also displays an alert message.
4. **When you find your iPhone (fingers crossed), tap the alert to silence the sound.**

Locking the data on your lost iPhone

If you can't find your iPhone right away by playing a sound, your next step should be to ensure that some other person who finds the phone can't rummage around in your stuff. You do that by putting your iPhone into Lost Mode, which remotely locks the iPhone using the passcode that you set earlier. (Sorry, if you didn't protect your iPhone with a passcode, you can't remotely lock your phone.) You can also provide a phone number where you can be reached and send a message for whoever finds your iPhone. Follow these steps to put your iPhone into Lost Mode:

1. **Display the My Devices list.**
2. **Tap or click your iPhone in the list.** The app locates your iPhone on a map.
3. **Enable Lost Mode:**
   - **Find My app.** In the Mark As Lost section, tap Activate and then tap Continue.
   - **iCloud.** Click Lost Mode.
4. **Enter a passcode (twice) to lock the iPhone.** You're prompted to enter a phone number where you can be reached.
5. **Type your phone number and then tap or click Next.** You're prompted to type a message that will appear on the iPhone along with the phone number.
6. **Type the message and then either tap Activate or click Done.** Find My iPhone remotely locks the iPhone and displays the message.

Deleting the data on your lost iPhone

If you can't get the other person to return your iPhone and it contains sensitive or confidential data — or just that big chunk of your life I mentioned earlier — you can use the Find My app or the iCloud Find My iPhone feature to take the drastic step of remotely wiping all the data from your iPhone. Here's what you do:

1. **Display the My Devices list.**
2. **Tap or click your iPhone in the list.** The app locates your iPhone on a map.
3. **Initiate the erase procedure:**
   - **Find My app.** Tap Erase This Device and then tap Continue.
   - **iCloud.** Click Erase iPhone, click Erase, type your Apple password, and then click Next.

   The app asks you to enter an optional phone number where you can be reached, which will appear on the iPhone after it has been erased.
4. **Type your phone number and then select Next.** The app prompts you to type a message that will appear on the iPhone along with the phone number, after it has been erased.
5. **Type the message and then either tap Erase or click Done.** The app remotely wipes all data from the iPhone.

How Do I Connect My iPhone to a Network?

As a standalone device, your iPhone works just fine, thank you, because you can make calls, listen to music, take pictures, record and edit video, work with your contacts and calendars, take notes, play games, and much more. But your iPhone was made to connect: to surf the web, exchange email and text messages, watch YouTube videos, navigate with maps, and on and on. To do all that, your iPhone must first connect to a network, and that's what this chapter is all about. I show you how to make, monitor, and control network connections; set up your iPhone as an Internet hub; and more.

Connecting to a Wi-Fi Network

Connections to a cellular network are automatic and occur behind the scenes. As soon as you switch on your iPhone, it checks for an LTE or 5G signal. If it finds one, it connects to the network and displays the LTE or 5G icon in the status bar, as well as the connection strength (the more bars, the better). If your current area doesn't do either LTE or 5G, your iPhone tries to connect to the slower 3G network. If that works, you see the 3G icon in the status bar and the connection strength. If there's no 3G network in sight, your iPhone tries to connect to a slower EDGE network instead. If that works, you see the E icon in the status bar (plus the usual signal strength bars). If none of that works, you see No Signal, so you might as well go home.

Making your first connection

Things aren't automatic when it comes to Wi-Fi connections, at least not at first. To see the list of available networks, you have two options:

- Display the Control Center, long press anywhere in the section that includes the Wi-Fi icon, and then tap and hold the Wi-Fi icon.
- Open the Settings app and then tap Wi-Fi.

Whichever method you use, you see a list of nearby networks, as shown in Figure 3.1.

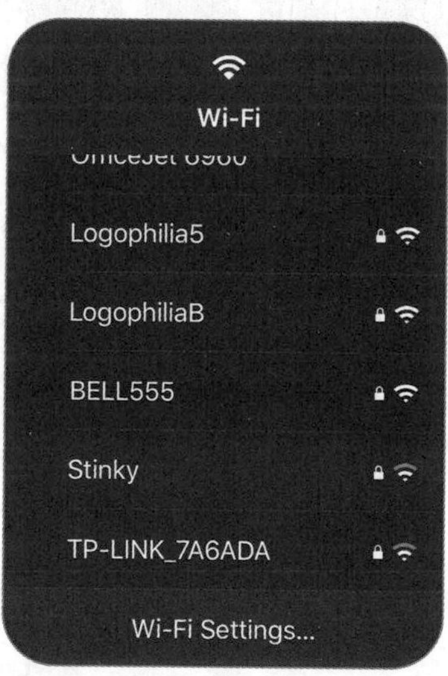

3.1 If you're just starting out on the Wi-Fi trail, get your iPhone to display a list of nearby networks.

For each network, you get three tidbits of data:

- **Network name.** This is the name that the administrator has assigned to the network. If you're in a coffee shop or similar public hotspot and you want to use that network, look for the name of the shop (or a variation on the name).
- **Password-protection.** If a Wi-Fi network displays a lock icon, it means that it's protected by a password, and you need that password to make the connection.
- **Signal strength.** This icon gives you a rough idea of how strong the wireless signals are. The stronger the signal (the more bars you see, the better the signal), the more likely you are to get a fast and reliable connection.

Follow these steps to connect to one of these Wi-Fi networks:

1. **Tap the network you want to use.** If the network is protected by a password, your iPhone prompts you to enter it.
2. **Type the password.**

Caution

Because the password box shows dots instead of the actual text for added security, this is no place to demonstrate your iPhone speed-typing prowess. Keep it slow and steady and note that the iPhone displays the actual character you type for about a second before changing it to a dot, so you can check your typing as you go.

3. **Tap Join.** The iPhone connects to the network and adds the Wi-Fi network signal strength icon to the status bar.

To connect to a commercial Wi-Fi operation — such as those you find in airports, hotels, and convention centers — you almost always have to take one more step. Usually, the network prompts you for your name and credit card data so you can be charged for accessing the network. If you're not prompted right away, you will be as soon as you try to access a web site or check your email. Enter your information and then enjoy the Internet in all its (expensive) Wi-Fi glory.

Showing available Wi-Fi networks automatically

If you're moving around town, having to constantly display the list of available Wi-Fi networks manually can become a pain. To ease that pain, you can configure your iPhone to display the list automatically.

Here's how:

1. **On the Home screen, tap Settings.** The Settings app appears.
2. **Tap Wi-Fi.** iPhone opens the Wi-Fi Networks screen.
3. **Tap Ask to Join Networks.** The Ask to Join Networks screen appears.
4. **Tap Ask.**

Genius

Rather than activating the Ask option in the Ask to Join Networks screen, an alternative is the Notify option. When you activate Notify, iOS only looks for nearby networks that are popular (that is, being accessed by many people). If iOS finds such a network, it displays a notification to let you know, and you can then tap Join to access the network.

Now, as soon as you try to access something on the Internet — a web site, your email, a map, or whatever — your iPhone scours the surrounding airwaves for Wi-Fi network signals. If you've never connected to a Wi-Fi network or if you're in an area that doesn't have any Wi-Fi networks that you've used in the past, you see the list of nearby wireless networks automatically. Sweet.

Connecting to known networks

Your iPhone remembers any Wi-Fi network to which you connect. So, if the network is one that you use all the time — for example, your home or office — your iPhone makes the connection without so much as a peep as soon as that network comes within range. Thanks!

Connecting to a hidden Wi-Fi network

Each Wi-Fi network has a network name — often called the Service Set Identifier, or SSID — that identifies the network to Wi-Fi–friendly devices, such as your iPhone. By default, most Wi-Fi networks broadcast the network name so that you can see it and connect to it. However, some Wi-Fi networks disable network name broadcasting as a security precaution. The idea here is that if an unauthorized user can't see the network, he or she can't attempt to connect to it. (However, some devices can still pick up the network name when authorized computers connect to it, so this is not a foolproof security measure.)

You can still connect to a hidden Wi-Fi network by entering the connection settings by hand. You need to know the network name, its security and encryption types, and the network password. Here are the steps to follow:

1. **On the Home screen, tap Settings to open the Settings app.**
2. **Tap Wi-Fi.** You see the Wi-Fi Networks screen.
3. **In the list of networks, tap Other.** Your iPhone displays the Other Network screen, as shown in Figure 3.2.
4. **Type the network name in the Name text box.**
5. **Tap Security to open the Security screen.**
6. **Tap the type of security the Wi-Fi network uses: None, WEP, WPA, WPA2/WPA3, WPA3, WPA Enterprise, WPA2 Enterprise, or WPA3 Enterprise.** If you're not sure, most secure networks use WPA2/WPA3.
7. **Tap Back to return to the Other Network screen.** If you chose a network security type other than None, your iPhone prompts you to type the password.
8. **Type the password in the Password text box.**
9. **Tap Join.** The iPhone connects to the network and adds the Wi-Fi network signal strength icon to the status bar.

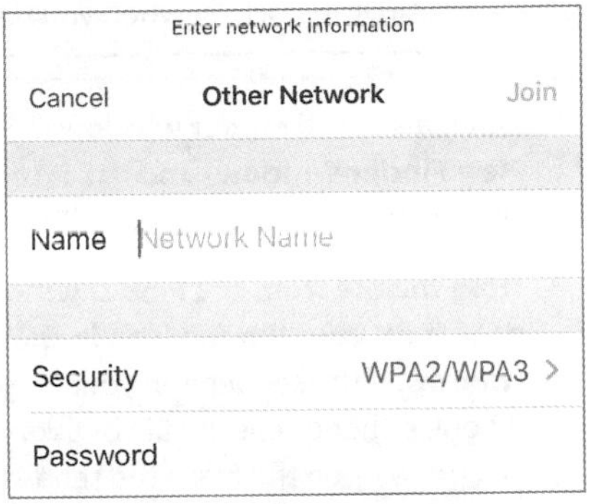

Enter network information

Cancel Other Network Join

Name Network Name

Security WPA2/WPA3 >

Password

3.2 Use the Other Network screen to connect to a hidden Wi-Fi network.

Sending a file from your Mac to your iPhone

If your Mac is running OS X Yosemite or later and your Mac and iPhone are connected to the same Wi-Fi network, you can use a tool called AirDrop to send a file directly from your Mac to your phone. Here's how it works:

1. **On your Mac, open Finder and click AirDrop in the sidebar.** You can also click Go → AirDrop or press cmd+Shift+R. You should see an icon for your iPhone in the AirDrop window.

Note

If you don't see your iPhone, make sure it has AirDrop turned on. Open the Settings app, tap General, tap AirDrop, and then tap Contacts Only. If you still don't see your iPhone on your Mac, tap Everyone instead. If you tap Everyone, then for security reasons you should tap Contacts Only after the transfer is complete. For even better security, tap Receiving Off; you can always turn AirDrop back on when you need it.

2. **Open a second Finder window (click File → New Finder Window) and use it to locate the file you want to send to your iPhone.**
3. **Drag the file from the Finder window and drop it on your iPhone icon in the AirDrop window.** If the sender is in your Contacts, your iPhone either opens the file or asks you to select an app to open the file; if the sender isn't in your Contacts, your iPhone asks you to confirm the transfer by tapping Accept.
4. **If your iPhone asks you to select an app to open the incoming file, as shown in Figure 3.3 (the file being transferred in this case is a PDF document), tap the app you want to use.** Alternatively, you can tap Save to iCloud Drive to save the file to the cloud instead of opening it. Your iPhone completes the transfer and displays or saves the file.

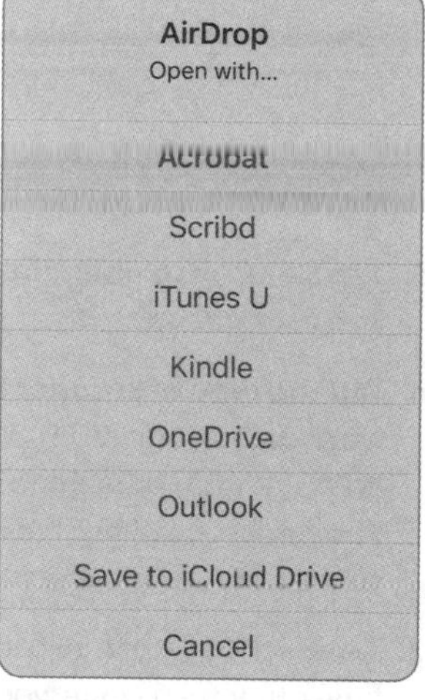

3.3 For some AirDrop transfers, your iPhone asks you to choose an app to open the file.

Forgetting a Wi-Fi network

Having the iPhone remember networks you've joined is certainly convenient, except, of course, when it's not. For example, if you have a couple of networks nearby that you can join, you might connect to one and then realize that the other is better in some way (for example, it's faster or cheaper). Unfortunately, there's a good chance your iPhone will continue to connect to the network you don't want every time it comes within range, which can be a real hassle. Rather than threatening to throw your iPhone in the nearest trash can, you can tell it to forget the network you don't want to use. Here's how it's done:

1. **On the Home screen, tap Settings.** The Settings app appears.
2. **Tap Wi-Fi.** The iPhone opens the Wi-Fi Networks screen.

3. **Tap the blue More Info icon to the right of the network you want to forget.** Your iPhone displays the network's settings screen.
4. **Tap Forget this Network.** Your iPhone asks you to confirm.
5. **Tap Forget.** Your iPhone discards the login data for the network and no longer connects to the network automatically.

Turning off the Wi-Fi antenna

The Wi-Fi antenna on your iPhone is constantly on the lookout for nearby Wi-Fi networks. That's useful because it means you always have an up-to-date list of networks to check out and it makes the iPhone location services (such as the Maps app) more accurate, but it also takes its toll on the iPhone battery. If you know you won't be using Wi-Fi for a while, you can save some battery juice for more important pursuits by turning off the Wi-Fi antenna. Here's how:

1. **On the Home screen, tap Settings.** The Settings app appears.
2. **Tap Wi-Fi.** The Wi-Fi Networks screen appears.
3. **Tap the Wi-Fi switch to Off.** Your iPhone disconnects from your current network and hides the Choose a Network list.

When you're ready to resume your Wi-Fi duties, return to the Wi-Fi Networks screen and tap the Wi-Fi switch to On.

Genius

You can also toggle the Wi-Fi antenna off and on by opening the Control Center and then tapping the Wi-Fi icon.

Setting Up Your iPhone as an Internet Hub

Here's a scenario you've probably tripped over a time or two when roaming around with both your iPhone and your notebook computer. You end up at a location where you have access to just a cellular network, with no Wi-Fi in sight. This means that your iPhone can access the Internet (using the cellular network), but your notebook can't. That's a real pain if you want to do some work involving Internet access on the computer. To work around this problem, you can use a nifty feature called Personal Hotspot, which enables you to configure your iPhone as a kind of Internet hub or gateway device — something like the hotspots that are available in coffee shops and other public areas. To do this, you connect your iPhone to your notebook (either directly via a USB cable or wirelessly via Wi-Fi or Bluetooth), and your notebook can then use the cellular Internet connection of your iPhone to get online. This is often called *Internet tethering*. Even better, you can connect up to five devices to your iPhone, so you can also share your iPhone Internet connection with desktop computers, tablets, other smartphones, and pretty much anything else that can connect to the Internet.

This sounds too good to be true, but it's real, I swear. The downside (you just knew there had to be a downside) is that some providers will charge you extra for tethering. This is slowly changing (for example, AT&T in the United States offers tethering on many of its smartphone plans), but you should read the fine print on your contract to be sure.

Activating the Personal Hotspot

Your first step down the Personal Hotspot road is to activate the feature. Here's how it's done:

1. **On the Home screen, tap Settings.** The Settings app appears.
2. **Tap Personal Hotspot.** iOS displays the Personal Hotspot settings.
3. **Tap the Allow Others to Join switch to On, as shown in Figure 3.4.**
4. **Tap Wi-Fi Password, type a password, and then tap Done.**

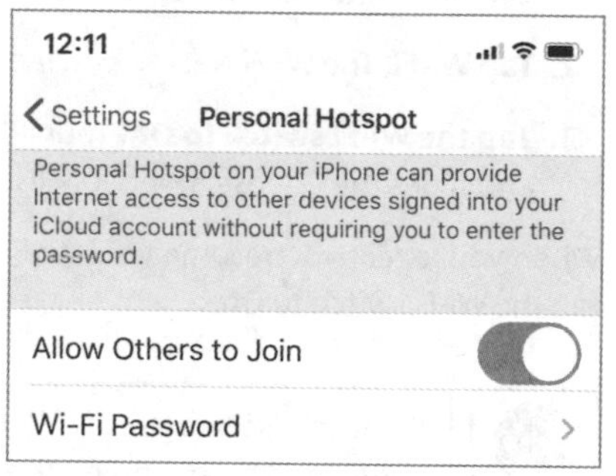

3.4 When the Allow Others to Join switch is On, other people or devices can connect to your iPhone's personal hotspot.

Connecting to the hotspot using Wi-Fi

With Personal Hotspot enabled, follow these steps to allow a device such as a Mac, a PC, or an iPad to use your iPhone Internet connection via Wi-Fi:

1. **On the device, display the list of nearby wireless networks.**
2. **In the network list, click the one that has the same name as your iPhone.** Your device prompts you for the Wi-Fi password.
3. **Type the Personal Hotspot Wi-Fi password and then click OK.** Your iPhone indicates one or more hotspot connections by showing the time with a blue background, as shown in Figure 3.5.

Genius

While the time is highlighted with the blue background, you can tap the time to go directly to the Personal Hotspot settings.

The time is highlighted when you have active hotspot connections

3.5 When you successfully set up a connection to the Personal Hotspot, the iPhone displays a banner showing you how many current connections you have.

Keeping an Eye on Your Data Usage

If you're using your iPhone with a plan that comes with a maximum amount of monthly data and you exceed that monthly cap, you'll almost certainly either pay big bucks for the privilege or have to deal with a slower connection speed. To avoid that, most cellular providers are kind enough to send you a message when you approach your cap. However, if you don't trust that process or if you're just paranoid about these things (justly, in my view), then you can keep an eye on your data usage yourself. Your iPhone keeps track of the cellular network data it has sent or received, as well as the roaming data it has sent or received if you've used your iPhone out of your coverage area.

First, take a look at your most recent bill from your cellular provider and, in particular, look for the dates the bill covers. For example, the bill might run from the 24th of one month to the 23rd of the next month. This is important because it tells you when you need to reset the usage data on your iPhone.

Now follow these steps to check your cellular data usage:

1. **On the Home screen, tap Settings.** The Settings app appears.
2. **Tap Cellular to open the Cellular screen.**
3. **In the Cellular Data section, read the Current Period and Current Period Roaming values.**
4. **If you're at the end of your data period, tap Reset Statistics at the bottom of the screen to start with fresh values for the new period.**

Controlling Network Data

Your iPhone gives you fairly precise control over your network data. For example, you can toggle just the LTE data, all cellular data, data for individual apps, data roaming, or all your iPhone antennas. The next few sections provide the details.

Turning off LTE

Using the LTE cellular network is a real pleasure because it's so much faster than a 3G connection (which in turn is much faster than a molasses-in-January EDGE connection). If LTE has a downside, it's that it uses up a lot of battery power. That's true even if you're currently connected to a Wi-Fi network, because the LTE antenna is constantly looking for an LTE signal. If you'll be on your Wi-Fi network for a while or if your battery is running low and you don't need an LTE cellular connection, you should turn off the LTE antenna to reduce the load on your iPhone battery. Here's how:

1. **On the Home screen, tap Settings.** The Settings app appears.
2. **Tap Cellular.** The Cellular screen opens.
3. **Tap Cellular Data Options.**
4. **Tap Voice & Data.** The Voice & Data screen opens.
5. **Tap 3G.** Your iPhone turns off the LTE antenna in favor of the lower-power 3G antenna.

Turning off cellular data

If you've reached the limit of your cellular data plan, you almost certainly want to avoid going over the cap because the charges are usually prohibitively expensive. As long as you have a Wi-Fi network in range or you're disciplined enough not to surf the web or cruise YouTube when there's no Wi-Fi in sight, you'll be okay. Still, accidents can happen. For example, you might accidentally tap a link in an email message or text message, or someone in your household might use your phone without knowing about your restrictions.

To prevent these sorts of accidents (or if you simply don't trust yourself when it comes to YouTube), you can turn off cellular data altogether, which means your iPhone accesses Internet data only if it has a Wi-Fi signal. Follow these steps to turn off cellular data on your iPhone:

1. **On the Home screen, tap Settings.** The Settings app appears.
2. **Tap Cellular.** The Cellular screen opens.
3. **Tap the Cellular Data switch to Off.**

Controlling cellular data usage

Rather than turning off cellular data completely, as I described in the previous section, you can take a more targeted approach. For example, if you're a bit worried about going over your cellular plan's data ceiling, it makes sense to avoid relatively high-bandwidth items, such as FaceTime and iTunes, but not relatively low-bandwidth content, such as iCloud documents and the Safari reading list.

You could just police this yourself, but, hey, you're a busy person, and you might forget the next time a FaceTime call comes in and you're in a cellular-only neighborhood. I say leave the details to your iPhone by configuring it to not allow certain apps and content types over a cellular connection. Here's how:

1. **On the Home screen, tap Settings.** The Settings app appears.
2. **Tap Cellular.** The Cellular screen opens.
3. **In the Cellular Data section, tap the switch to Off for each app or type of content you want to ban from cellular (see Figure 3.6).**

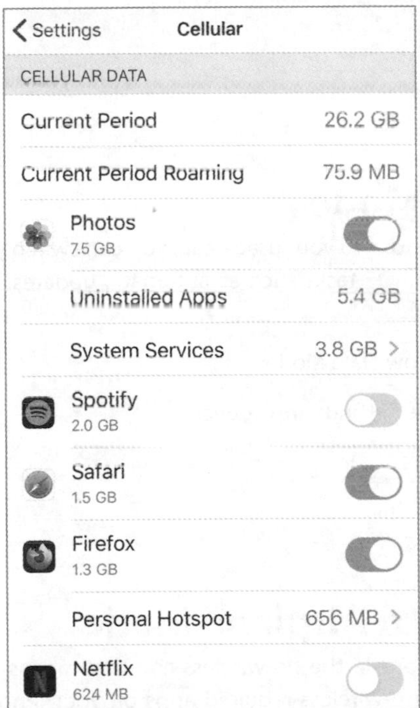

3.6 You can configure your iPhone to not use certain apps or types of content over the cellular network.

Turning off data roaming

Data roaming is an often-convenient cell phone feature that enables you to make calls — and, with your iPhone, surf the web, check and send email, and exchange text messages — when you're outside of your normal coverage area. The downside is that, unless you've got a fixed-rate roaming package from your cellular provider, roaming charges are almost always eye-poppingly expensive. You're often talking several dollars per minute or megabyte, depending on where you are and what type of service you're using. Not good!

Unfortunately, if you have the Data Roaming feature on your iPhone turned on, you may incur massive roaming charges even if you never use your phone! That's because your iPhone still performs background checks for things like incoming email messages and text messages, so a week in some far off land could cost you hundreds of dollars without even using your phone.

To avoid this insanity, turn off the Data Roaming feature on your iPhone when you don't need it. Follow these steps:

1. **On the Home screen, tap Settings.** The Settings app appears.
2. **Tap Cellular.** The Cellular screen appears.
3. **Tap Cellular Data Options.**
4. **Tap the Data Roaming switch to Off.**

Switching to Low Data Mode

If your cellular data is getting dangerously close to your usage cap, you can switch your iPhone into Low Data Mode, which pauses iOS tasks such as automatic updates, and background tasks, such as photo syncing.

Follow these steps to put your iPhone into Low Data Mode:

1. **On the Home screen, tap Settings.** The Settings app appears.
2. **Tap Cellular.** The Cellular screen appears.
3. **Tap Cellular Data Options.**
4. **Tap the Low Data Mode switch to On.**

Switching your iPhone to Airplane Mode

When you board a flight, how do you reconcile the no-wireless-and-that-means-you airlines regulations with the multitude of no-wireless-required apps on your iPhone? You put your iPhone into a special state called Airplane Mode. This mode turns off the transceivers — the internal components that transmit and receive wireless signals — for the phone, Wi-Fi, and Bluetooth features. With your iPhone now safely in compliance with federal aviation regulations, you're free to use any app that doesn't rely on wireless transmissions.

Caution

If you switch to Airplane Mode and then turn on Wi-Fi or Bluetooth (or both), iOS remembers this and turns on those transceivers the next time you switch to Airplane Mode. Having either or both of these radios turned on might not be allowed by your current airline, so double-check whether any transceivers are still active each time you switch to Airplane Mode.

There are two methods you can use to activate Airplane Mode:

- **On the Home screen, tap Settings and then tap the Airplane Mode switch to On.**
- **Open the Control Center and then tap the Airplane Mode button.**

Your iPhone disconnects your cellular network and your wireless network (if you have a current connection). Notice, as well, that while Airplane Mode is on, an Airplane Mode icon appears in the status bar in place of the Signal Strength and Network icons (see Figure 3.7).

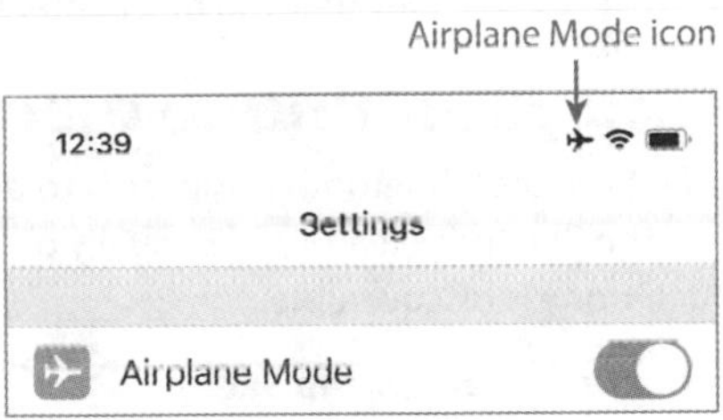

3.7 When your iPhone is in Airplane Mode, an Airplane Mode icon appears in the status bar.

Pairing Your iPhone to Bluetooth Devices

Your iPhone is configured to use a wireless technology called Bluetooth, which enables you to make wireless connections to other Bluetooth-friendly devices. Most Macs come with Bluetooth built in, and they use it to connect to a wide range of devices, including mice, keyboards, cell phones, printers, digital cameras, other Macs, and even the new iPhone-compatible game controllers that were about to come to market as this book went to press. Your iPhone can, at the very least, connect to a Bluetooth headset on which you can listen to phone conversations, music, and movies without wires and without disturbing your neighbors.

In theory, connecting Bluetooth devices should be criminally easy: You bring them within 33 feet of each other (the maximum Bluetooth range), and they connect without further ado. In practice, however, there's usually at least a bit of further ado (and sometimes plenty of it). This usually takes one or both of the following forms:

- **Making the devices discoverable.** Unlike Wi-Fi devices that broadcast their signals constantly, most Bluetooth devices broadcast their availability — that is, they make themselves *discoverable* — only when you say so. This makes sense in many cases because you usually only want to connect a Bluetooth component, such as a headset, with a single device. By controlling when the device is discoverable, you ensure that it works only with the device you want it to.
- **Pairing the iPhone and the device.** As a security precaution, many Bluetooth devices need to be *paired* with another device before the connection is established. Usually, the pairing is accomplished by entering a multidigit *passkey* — your iPhone calls it a PIN — that you must then enter into the Bluetooth device (assuming, of course, that it has some kind of keypad). In the case of a headset, the device comes with a default passkey that you must enter into your iPhone to set up the pairing.

Making your iPhone discoverable

So your first order of Bluetooth business is to ensure that your iPhone is discoverable by activating the Bluetooth feature. It is usually on by default, but follow these steps to make sure your iPhone is discoverable:

1. **On the Home screen, tap Settings.** The Settings app appears.
2. **Tap Bluetooth.** The Bluetooth screen appears.
3. **Tap the Bluetooth switch to On, as shown in Figure 3.8.**

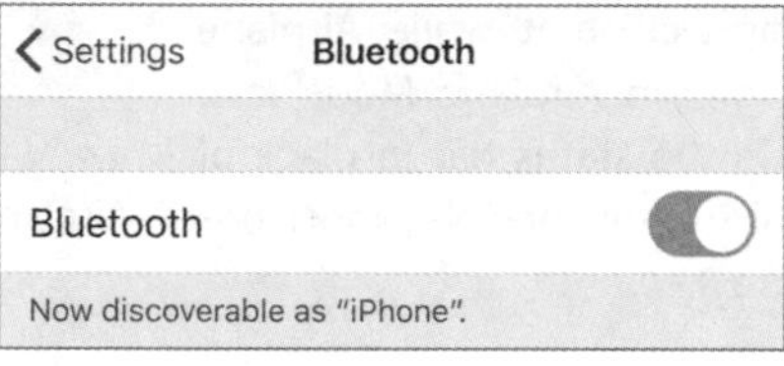

3.8 Use the Bluetooth screen to make your iPhone discoverable.

Pairing your iPhone with a Bluetooth keyboard

The iPhone virtual keyboard is an ingenious invention, but it's not always a convenient one, particularly when you need to type fast or type a lot. Fortunately, iOS supports connections to a Bluetooth keyboard that, while paired, disables the on-screen keyboard. Follow these steps to pair your iPhone with a Bluetooth keyboard:

1. **On the Home screen, tap Settings.** The Settings app appears.
2. **Tap Bluetooth.** The Bluetooth screen appears.

3. **If the keyboard has a separate switch or button that makes the device discoverable, turn on that switch or press that button.** Wait until you see the keyboard appear in the Bluetooth screen.

4. **Tap the name of the Bluetooth keyboard.** Your iPhone displays a passkey, as shown in Figure 3.9.

5. **On the Bluetooth keyboard, type the passkey and press Return or Enter.** Your iPhone pairs with the keyboard and returns you to the Bluetooth screen, where you now see *Connected* beside the keyboard.

Bluetooth Pairing Request

Enter this code on "Microsoft Bluetooth Mobile Keyboard 6000", followed by the return or enter key.

4118

Cancel

3.9 Your iPhone displays a passkey, which you then type on the Bluetooth keyboard.

Pairing your iPhone with a Bluetooth headset

If you want to listen to music, headphones are a great way to go because the sound is often better than with the built-in iPhone speakers (and no one else around is subjected to The Black Keys at top volume). Similarly, if you want to conduct a hands-free call, a headset (a combination of headphones for listening and a microphone for talking) makes life easier because you can put the phone down and make all the hand gestures you want (provided you aren't driving, of course). Add Bluetooth into the mix, and you've got an easy and wireless audio solution for your iPhone.

Follow these general steps to pair your iPhone with a Bluetooth headset:

1. **On the Home screen, tap Settings.** The Settings app appears.

2. **Tap Bluetooth.** The Bluetooth screen appears.

3. **If the headset has a separate switch or button that makes the device discoverable, turn on that switch or press that button.** Wait until you see the correct headset name appear in the Bluetooth screen.

4. **Tap the name of the Bluetooth headset.** Your iPhone should pair with the headset automatically, and you should see *Connected* in the Bluetooth screen. If you see this, you can skip the rest of these steps. Otherwise, you see the Enter PIN screen.

5. **Enter the headset's passkey in the PIN box.** See the headset documentation to get the passkey (it's often 0000).

6. **Tap Done.** Your iPhone pairs with the headset and returns you to the Bluetooth screen, where you now see *Connected* beside the headset name.

Selecting a paired headset as the audio output device

After you pair a Bluetooth headset, your iPhone is usually smart enough to start blasting your tunes through the headset instead of the phone's built-in speaker. If that doesn't happen, follow these steps to choose your Bluetooth headset as the output device:

1. **Open the Control Center.**
2. **Tap the AirPlay icon that appears in the top-right corner of the playback controls.** The AirPlay screen appears.
3. **Tap your paired Bluetooth headset.** You see a check mark beside the headset, as shown in Figure 3.10, and your iPhone starts playing audio through the headset.

3.10 Use the AirPlay screen to select your paired Bluetooth headset.

Unpairing your iPhone from a Bluetooth device

If you no longer plan to use a Bluetooth device, you should unpair it from your iPhone. Follow these steps:

1. **On the Home screen, tap Settings.** The Settings app appears.
2. **Tap Bluetooth.** The Bluetooth screen appears.
3. **Tap the blue More Info icon to the right of the Bluetooth device name.**
4. **Tap Forget this Device.** Your iPhone unpairs the device.

How Can I Get More Out of the Phone App?

1 2 3 4 5 6 7 8 9 10 11

The iPhone is chock-full of great apps that enable you to surf the web, send and receive email messages, listen to music, take photos, organize your contacts, schedule appointments, and much, much more. These features put the *smart* in its status as a *smartphone*, but let's not forget the *phone* part! So, while you're probably familiar with the basic steps required to make and answer calls, the powerful phone component in your iPhone is loaded with amazing features that can make the cell phone portion of your life easier, more convenient, and more efficient. This chapter takes you through these features.

Working with Outgoing Calls

You can do much more with your iPhone than just make a call the old-fashioned way — by dialing the phone number. There are speedy shortcuts you can take, and even settings to alter the way your outgoing calls look on the receiver's phone.

Note

If you're getting low on minutes with your cellular plan, you might still be able to make a call without using up what little time you have left. That's because iOS supports *Wi-Fi calling*, which enables you to place a call using a Wi-Fi Internet connection instead of a cellular connection. Check with your cellular provider to see if it supports Wi-Fi calling. To turn on Wi-Fi calling, open Settings, tap Phone, tap Wi-Fi Calling, then tap the Wi-Fi Calling on This iPhone switch to On.

Making calls quickly

The iPhone has a seemingly endless number of methods you can use to make a call. It's nice to have the variety, but in this have-your-people-call-my-people world, the big question is not how many ways can you make a call, but how *fast* can you make a call? Here are my favorite iPhone speed-calling techniques:

- **Favorites list.** This list acts as a kind of speed dial for the iPhone because you use it to store the phone numbers you call most often, and you have space to add your top 20 numbers. To call someone in your Favorites list, tap the Phone icon on the Home screen, tap Favorites, and then tap the number you want to call. I show you how to manage your Favorites later in this chapter.
- **Visual Voicemail.** If you're checking your voicemail messages (from the Home screen, tap Phone and then tap Voicemail) and you want to return someone's call, tap the message and then tap Call Back.
- **Text message.** If someone includes a phone number in a text message, your iPhone handily converts it into a link. The number appears in blue text, much like a link on a web page, as shown in Figure 4.1. Tap the phone number to call it. You can also use a similar technique to call numbers embedded in web pages (see Chapter 5) and email messages (see Chapter 6).

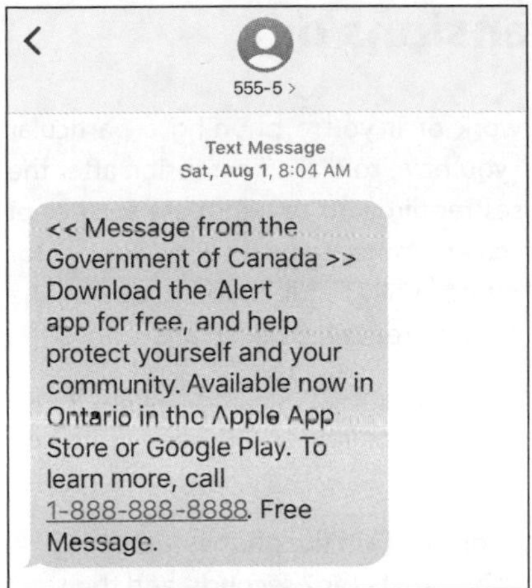

4.1 Your iPhone is kind enough to convert a phone number in a text message into a link that you can tap to call.

Note

You can do a lot more than just call a number in a text message. Tap the contact image at the top of the screen and then tap the Info icon to see a menu of actions you can take with the phone number, including sending the person your location, initiating a FaceTime call, creating a new contact, and adding the number to an existing contact.

- **Recent numbers.** The Recent Calls list (from the Home screen, tap Phone and then tap Recents) shows your recent phone activity: calls you've made, calls you've received, and calls you've missed. Recent Calls is great because it enables you to quickly redial someone with whom you've had recent contact. To call the person using a different phone number, tap the Info icon (the arrow to the right of the name or number), and then tap the phone number you want to use to make the call. If you want to return a missed call, tap Missed and then tap the call.

Genius

If your Recent Calls list is populated with names or numbers that you know you won't ever call back, you should either remove those numbers or clear the list and start fresh. In the Recent screen, tap Edit. To remove a number, tap the red delete button to the left of the number and then tap Delete. To start anew, tap Clear and then tap Clear All Recents.

Automatically dialing extensions or menu options

If you're calling a family member or friend at work or if you're phoning a particular department or person in a company, chances are you have to dial an extension after the main number connects. Similarly, many businesses require you to negotiate a series of menus to get information or connect with a particular employee or section ("Press 1 for Sales; press 2 for Customer Service," and so on). This normally requires you to display the keyboard, listen for the prompts, enter the numbers, and repeat as necessary.

However, if you know the extension or phone menu sequence, you can program it into the number and have the Phone app do all the hard work for you. The Phone app can do either of the following:

- **Pause.** This option, which is represented by a comma (,) in the phone number, means that the Phone app dials the main number, waits for 2 seconds, and then dials whatever extension or menu value appears after the comma. You can add multiple commas to the number if you need a longer delay.
- **Wait.** This option, which is represented by a semicolon (;) in the phone number, means that the Phone app dials just the main number and also displays a button labeled Dial "*extension*," where *extension* is whatever digits appear after the semicolon. When the phone system prompts you to enter the extension, just tap the Dial button.

You can set these up in two ways:

- **Contacts list.** When you're entering a phone number using the Contacts list, type the full number and then tap the +*# key that appears in the lower-left corner of the on-screen keyboard. This temporarily adds two new keys: Pause and Wait. Tap Pause to add a comma, then tap the extension or menu value, and repeat as needed; tap Wait to add a semicolon and then tap the extension.
- **Keypad.** Using the keypad in the Phone app, type the full number. To add a comma to tell the Phone app to pause, tap and hold the * key until a comma appears and then tap the extension or menu value; to add a semicolon to tell the Phone app to wait, tap and hold the # key until a semicolon appears and then tap the extension.

Voice dialing a call with Siri

Tapping a favorite number, a recent number, or a text message phone number link is a pretty easy method to launch a phone call, but there's an even easier way that doesn't require a single tap on your part. I speak, of course, of voice dialing, which is yet another hat worn by Siri, the voice-activated assistant. To voice dial, you tell Siri the name of the person you want to call (if she's in your Contacts list) or the number you want to call (for everyone else), and Siri does the rest. Here are the details:

1. **Say "Hey Siri" or tap and hold the Home button.** You can also press and hold the center button of the iPhone headset. The Siri screen appears.
2. **Say "Call" (or "Phone" or "Telephone" or "Dial") and then specify who or what:**
   - **If the person is in your Contacts list, say the person's first and last names.** If the contact is a business, say "*company*," where *company* is the business name as given in your Contacts list. If you have multiple numbers for the contact, also say the label of that number (such as "mobile" or "home"). If you're not sure of the correct label, skip that part and Siri will let you know which labels are available.
   - **If the person is in your Contacts list and has a unique first name, say the person's first name.**
   - **If the person has a relationship with you that you've defined with Siri, say "*relationship*," where *relationship* is the connection you've defined (such as brother or mother).**
   - **If you want to call one of your own numbers, say "Call *label*," where *label* is the label of the number in your Contacts data that you want to call.**
   - **For anyone else, say the full phone number you want to dial.**

Genius

You can be fairly casual about the syntax you use when specifying a label. For example, you can say something like "Call Belinda Gray at home" or "Call my sister on her mobile phone."

3. **If the person has multiple numbers and you didn't specify a label, Siri displays a list of the available numbers, as shown in Figure 4.2.** You now need to say the label of the number you want to dial. Conveniently, Siri also responds verbally by listing the available labels for that person, so you don't have to guess which one to use.

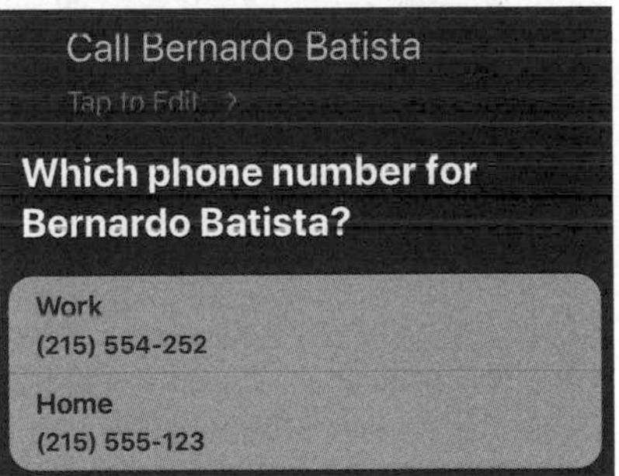

4.2 You see this screen if the person you're calling has multiple numbers and you don't specify a label.

That's it. For a contact, Siri responds with "Calling *name label*" (where *name* is the person's name and *label* is the label assigned to the phone number). For a phone number, Siri responds with "Calling *number*" (where *number* is the phone number you specified).

Configuring your iPhone not to show your caller ID

When you use your iPhone to call someone, and the called phone supports caller ID, your number and often your name appear. If you'd rather hide your identity for some reason, you can configure your iPhone not to show your caller ID:

1. **On the Home screen, tap Settings.** The Settings app appears.
2. **Tap Phone.** The Phone screen appears.
3. **Tap Show My Caller ID.** The Show My Caller ID screen appears.
4. **Tap the Show My Caller ID switch to Off.** Your iPhone disables caller ID.

Caution

You might have good reasons to hide your caller ID when making a call, but just beware that many people automatically ignore incoming calls that don't specify the caller's name (the reasonable assumption being that someone who hides their caller ID is likely up to no good).

Handling Incoming Calls

When a call comes in to your iPhone, you answer it, right? What could be simpler? You'd be surprised. Your iPhone gives you quite a few options for dealing with that call, aside from just answering it. After all, you don't want to talk to everyone all the time, do you?

Answering a call on other devices

It has happened to all of us: You're in one room when you hear your iPhone ring in another room, and a mad dash ensues to answer the call before it goes to voicemail. However, if you happen to have your iPad or even your Mac nearby, that mad dash need not take place. That's because iOS supports a feature that enables you to answer incoming calls on your other devices, including iPads, iPhones, and even Macs. Follow these steps to ensure this feature is activated and to control which devices you can use to answer calls:

1. **On the Home screen, tap Settings to open the Settings app.**
2. **Tap Phone to display the Phone settings.**

3. **Tap Calls on Other Devices.** Settings displays the Calls on Other Devices screen.
4. **Tap the Allow Calls on Other Devices switch to On.**
5. **In the list of devices that appears, tap the switch to Off for any device that you don't want to receive calls.**

Sending an incoming call directly to voicemail

Sometimes you just don't want to talk to someone. Whether that person is your sister calling to complain, an acquaintance who never seems to have anything to say, or someone who calls while you're indisposed, you might prefer to ignore the call.

That's not a problem on your iPhone because it gives you several ways to decline a call:

- If the phone isn't locked, tap the red Decline button on the touchscreen. (If your iPhone is locked, you don't see the Decline button.)
- If you're using the EarPods, squeeze and hold the center button for 2 seconds.
- Press the Sleep/Wake button twice in quick succession.

Each of these methods sends the call directly to voicemail.

Note

If you ignore a call, as with any phone, the caller will know that you've done so when voicemail kicks in before the normal four rings. If you don't want someone to know you're ignoring his or her call, press the Sleep/Wake button once to silence the ring. The caller still hears the standard four rings before the voicemail and will be none the wiser that you just didn't pick up your phone.

Replying with a message

In the previous section, you learned how to send an unwanted call directly to voicemail. That's great for calls you want to ignore, but there are plenty of situations where you can't answer the phone, but you also don't want to ignore the caller. For example, if you're expecting a call but get dragged into a meeting in the meantime, it would be rude to still answer the call when it comes in, but if you just send the call to voicemail, your caller might wonder what's going on. Similarly, you might be a bit late for an appointment, and on your way there you see a call come in from the person you're meeting. Again, it might not be convenient to answer the call, but letting voicemail handle it might lead your caller to wonder if you're going to show up for the meeting.

iOS offers a feature that gives you an easy way to handle these sticky phone situations. It's called Respond with Text, and it enables you to simultaneously decline a call *and* send the caller a prefab text message. That way, you avoid a voice conversation (which, depending on your current situation, might be rude or inconvenient), but you give the caller some feedback.

By default, Respond with Text comes with three ready-to-send messages:

Sorry, I can't talk right now.

I'm on my way.

Can I call you later?

There's also an option to send a custom message if none of these is quite right. Here's how to decline an incoming call and send the caller a text message:

1. **When the call comes in, tap Message, shown in Figure 4.3.** Your iPhone displays a button for each of the prefab text messages.

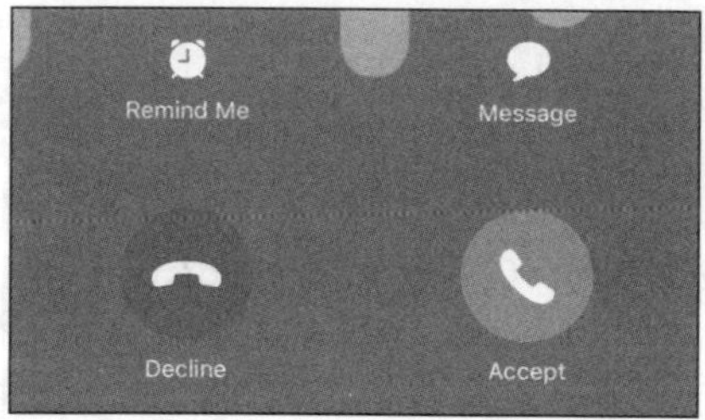

4.3 Tap Message to reply to the caller with a text message.

2. **Tap the reply you want to send.** If you want to send a different message, tap Custom, type your message, and then tap Send.

The caller sees User Busy in the Phone app and then receives a text message.

Note

You must have call display on your phone plan to see the Message button.

Genius

If you're not all that fond of the default replies, you can forge your own. Tap Settings, tap Phone, tap Respond with Text, and then use the three text boxes to type your own messages. Alternatively, when the call comes in, tap Message and then tap Custom.

Setting a callback reminder

The Respond with Text feature is a handy trick to have up your iPhone sleeve, but it suffers from the same problem that plagues straight-up declining a call: If you want to talk to that person later, you have to *remember* to call back. Fortunately, the Phone app has a feature that lets you decline a call and automatically create a callback reminder. You can set up the reminder to fire in one hour or when you leave your current location.

Here's how to decline an incoming call and set a callback reminder:

1. **When the call comes in, tap Remind Me.** Your iPhone displays the callback reminder options.
2. **Tap In 1 hour.** iOS sets a reminder using your default Reminders list.

Genius

Rather than declining all incoming calls, you might be in a situation where you want to decline all calls *except* for those from a particular person or group. A better way to handle this is to set up the Do Not Disturb feature to allow calls from just those people. For more details, see Chapter 2.

Turning off the call waiting feature

If you're already on a call and another one comes in, your iPhone springs into action and displays the person's name or number, as well as three options: Decline Incoming Call, Answer & Hold Current Call, and Answer & End Current Call. (See the section about handling multiple calls later in this chapter for more information about these options.) This is part of the Call Waiting feature on your iPhone, and it's great if you're expecting an important call or if you want to add the caller to a conference call that you've set up.

However, the rest of the time you might just find it annoying and intrusive (and anyone you put on hold or hang up on to take the new call probably finds it rude and insulting). In that case, you can turn off Call Waiting by following these steps:

1. **On the Home screen, tap Settings.** The Settings app appears.
2. **Tap Phone.** The Phone screen appears.
3. **Tap Call Waiting.** The Call Waiting screen appears.
4. **Tap the Call Waiting switch to Off.** Your iPhone disables Call Waiting.

Blocking incoming calls

Using your iPhone is a blast *until* you get your first call from a telemarketer, cold-calling salesperson, or someone similarly annoying. Happily, iOS offers the welcome ability to block certain people from calling you. If you're getting unwanted calls from an old flame, an old schoolmate, or anyone else you used to know but no longer want to, you can follow these steps to block those calls:

1. **On the Home screen, tap Settings to open the Settings app.**
2. **Tap Phone to display the Phone settings.**
3. **Tap Blocked Contacts to open the Blocked screen.**
4. **Tap Add New.** (If you already have some blocked callers, scroll to the bottom of the list to see the Add New command.) Your Contacts list appears.
5. **Tap the person you want to block.** Your iPhone adds that person's phone numbers and email address to the Blocked list.

Note

The blocking feature also applies to FaceTime calls and to text messages. So, an alternative method for adding someone to the Blocked list is to open Settings, tap Messages, tap Blocked Contacts, tap Add New, and then tap the person in your Contacts list.

What about people *not* in your Contacts list? No problem. Open the Phone app, tap Recents, and then tap the blue Info icon to the right of any call placed by the person you want to block. In the Info screen, tap Block this Caller and then tap Block Contact when you're asked to confirm.

Forwarding calls to another number

What do you do about incoming calls if you can't use your iPhone for a while? For example, if you're going on a flight, you must either turn off your iPhone or put it in Airplane mode (as described in Chapter 3) so incoming calls won't go through. Similarly, if you have to return your iPhone to Apple for repairs or battery replacement, the phone won't be available if anyone tries to call you.

For these and other situations where your iPhone can't accept incoming calls, you can work around the problem by having your calls forwarded to another number, such as your work or home number. Here's how it's done:

1. **On the Home screen, tap Settings.** The Settings app appears.
2. **Tap Phone.** The Phone screen appears.
3. **Tap Call Forwarding.** The Call Forwarding screen appears.
4. **Tap the Call Forwarding switch to On.** Your iPhone displays the Forward To command.

5. **Tap Forward To.** iOS displays the Forward To screen.
6. **Tap the phone number to use for the forwarded calls.**
7. **Tap Back to return to the Call Forwarding screen.**

Juggling Multiple Calls and Conference Calls

We all juggle multiple tasks and duties these days, so it's not surprising that sometimes this involves juggling multiple phone calls:

- You might need to call two people on a related issue and then switch back and forth between the callers as the negotiations (or whatever) progress.
- You might already be on a call and another call comes in from a person you need to speak to. So you put the initial person on hold, deal with the new caller, and then return to the first person.
- You might need to speak to two people at the same time on the same phone call — in other words, a conference call.

In the real world, juggling multiple calls and setting up conference calls often requires a special phone or a fancy phone system. In the iPhone world, however, these things are a snap. In fact, the way the iPhone juggles multiple calls really is something spectacular. Jumping back and forth between calls is simple, putting someone on hold to answer an incoming call is a piece of cake, and creating a conference call from incoming or outgoing calls is criminally easy.

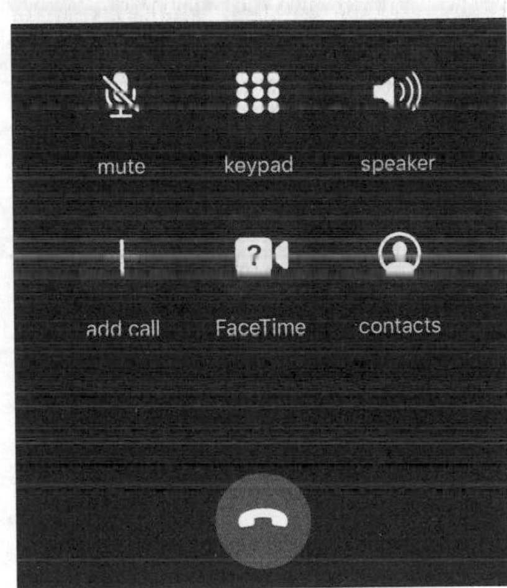

4.4 When you're on a call, your iPhone displays these call options.

When you're on an initial call, your iPhone displays the Call Options screen, as shown in Figure 4.4. To make another call, tap Add Call and then use the Phone app to place your second call.

You may be wondering how you put a phone call on hold. For reasons that remain mysterious, your iPhone hides this useful feature. To see it, press and hold the mute button, shown in Figure 4.4. After several seconds, your iPhone replaces this icon with a hold icon and puts the caller on hold. To take the caller off hold, tap that icon.

Once the second call goes through, the Call Options screen changes: The top of the screen shows the first caller's name (or number) with HOLD beside it, and below that you see the name (or number) of the second caller and the duration of that call. Figure 4.5 shows the new screen layout. To switch to the person on hold, tap the swap button. iPhone puts the second caller on hold and returns you to the first caller. Congratulations! You now have two calls going at once.

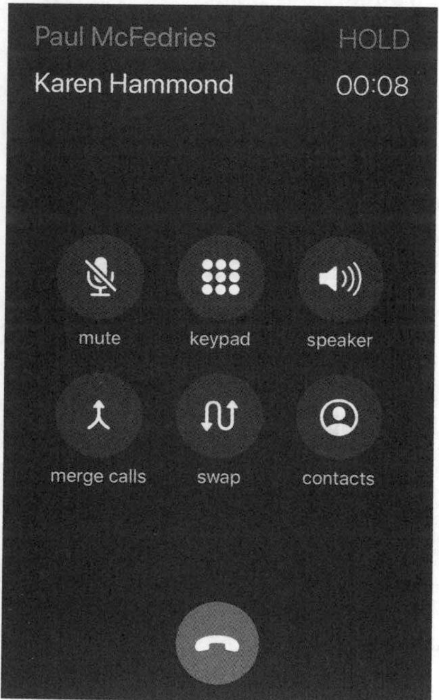

4.5 The iPhone Call Options screen with two phone calls on the go.

If you have two calls going, you might prefer that all three of you be able to talk to each other in a conference call. Easier done than said — just tap the Merge Calls option. iPhone combines everyone into a single conference call and displays Conference at the top of the Call Options screen. Tap the Info arrow and iPhone displays the participants' names (or numbers) in the Conference screen, as shown in Figure 4.6.

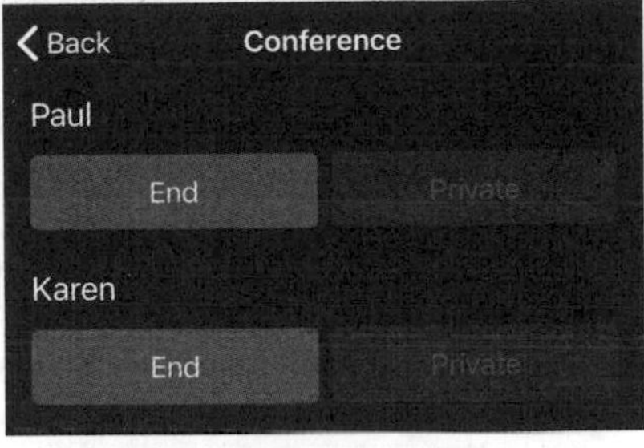

4.6 When you merge two phone calls, the participants' names or numbers appear in the Conference screen.

From here, there are a few methods you can use to manage your conference call:

- **To speak with one of the callers privately, tap the Private key below that person's name or number.** This places you in a one-on-one call with that person and places the other caller on hold.
- **To drop someone from the conference call, tap the End key below that person's name or number.** Your iPhone drops that caller, and you resume a private call with the other party.
- **To add someone else to the conference call, tap Back to return to the Call Options screen.** Tap Add Call and then make the call. Once the call goes through, tap Merge Calls.

Caution

You can hold a conference call with up to five people at once by repeating the steps outlined for conference calls. However, remember that conference calls use up your minutes faster — two callers use them up twice as fast, three callers use them up three times as fast, and so on — so you may want to be judicious when using this feature.

Managing Your Favorites List

The Favorites list on your iPhone is great for making quick calls because you can often get someone on the horn in just three finger gestures (from the Home screen, tap Phone, tap Favorites, and then tap the number). Of course, this works only if the numbers you call most often appear on your Favorites list. Fortunately, your iPhone gives you a lot of different ways to populate the list. Here are the easiest methods to use:

- **In the Favorites list, tap + to open the All Contacts screen and then tap the person you want to add.** If that person has multiple phone numbers, tap the number you want to use as a favorite. When the iPhone asks how you want to call the person, tap Voice Call, FaceTime Audio, or FaceTime.

Note

This is a good place to remind you that the Favorites list isn't a list of people; it's a list of numbers. That's why the list shows both the person's name and the type of phone number (work, home, mobile, and so on).

- **In the Recent Calls list, tap the More Info icon to the right of the call from (or to) the person you want to add and then tap Add to Favorites.** If the person has multiple phone numbers, tap the number you want to use as the favorite, and then tap Voice Call, FaceTime Audio, or FaceTime. iPhone adds a star beside the phone number to remind you that it's a favorite.
- **In Visual Voicemail, tap the More Info icon beside a message, tap Add to Favorites, and then tap Voice Call, FaceTime Audio, or FaceTime.**
- **In the Contacts list, tap the person you want to add and then tap Add to Favorites.** If the person has multiple phone numbers, tap the number you want to use as the favorite, and then tap Voice Call, FaceTime Audio, or FaceTime. iPhone adds a star beside the phone number to remind you that it's a favorite.

You can add up to 20 numbers in the Favorites list, but the iPhone screen shows only 8 at a time. This means that if you want to call someone who doesn't appear in the initial screen, you need to scroll down to bring that number into view. Therefore, your Favorites list is most efficient when the people you call most often appear in the first eight numbers. Your iPhone adds each new number to the bottom of the Favorites list, so chances are that at least some of your favorite numbers aren't showing up in the top eight. Follow these steps to fix that:

1. **In the Favorites list, tap Edit.** Your iPhone displays Delete icons to the left of each favorite and Drag icons to the right, as shown in Figure 4.7.
2. **If you want to get rid of a favorite, tap its Delete icon.**
3. **To move a favorite to a new location, tap and drag the Drag icon up or down until the favorite is where you want it; then release the icon.**
4. **Tap Done.**

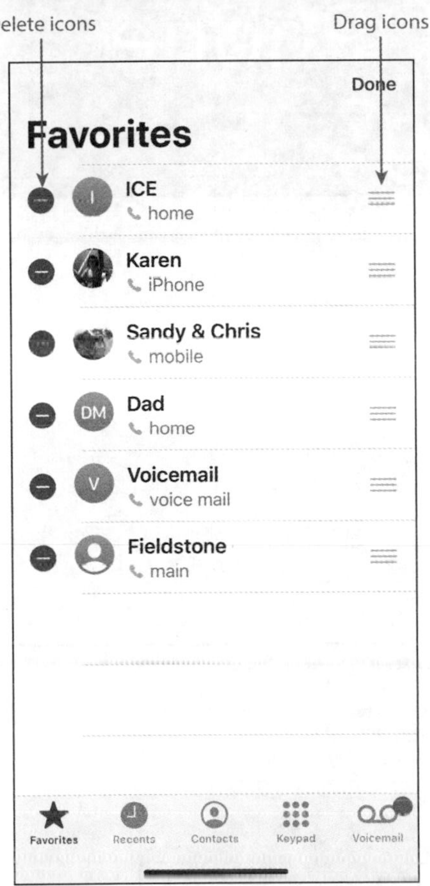

4.7 In Edit mode, the Favorites list shows Delete icons on the left and Drag icons on the right.

How Can I Make the Most of iPhone Web Surfing?

One of the most popular modern pastimes is web surfing, and now you can surf even when you're out and about thanks to the large screen on your iPhone and support for speedy networks, such as 5G, LTE, and Wi-Fi. You perform these surfin' safaris using, appropriately enough, the Safari web browser app, which is easy to use and intuitive. However, the Safari app offers quite a few options and features, many of which are hidden in obscure nooks and crannies of the iPhone interface. If you think your surfing activities could be faster, more efficient, more productive, or more secure, this chapter can help.

Touchscreen Tips for Web Sites

The touchscreen operates much the same way in Safari as it does in the other iPhone apps. You can use it to scroll pages, zoom in and out, tap links, fill in forms, enter addresses, and more. Here's a little collection of touchscreen tips that ought to make your web excursions even easier:

- **Double-tap.** A quick way to zoom in on a page that has various sections is to double-tap the specific section — it could be an image, a paragraph, a table, or a column of text — that you want magnified. Your iPhone zooms the section to fill the width of the screen. Double-tap again to return the page to the regular view.

Note

The double-tap-to-zoom trick works only on pages that have identifiable sections. If a page is just a wall of text, you can double-tap until the cows come home (that's a long time) and nothing much happens.

- **One tap to the top.** If you're reading a particularly long-winded web page and you're near the bottom, you may have quite a long way to scroll if you need to head back to the top to get at the address/search bar. Save the wear and tear on your flicking finger! Instead, tap the status bar at the top of the screen; Safari immediately transports you to the top of the page.

Genius

You might find it hard to reach the top of the screen if you're surfing one-handed. If your iPhone has a notch, swipe down from the bottom part of the screen to drop the Safari screen down halfway and bring its top bar within easy reach. If your iPhone has a Home button, you can drop down the screen by lightly double-tapping the Home button.

- **Tap and hold to see where a link takes you.** You "click" a link in a web page by tapping it with your finger. In a regular web browser, you can see where a link takes you (that is, the URL) by hovering the mouse pointer over the link and checking out the link address in the status bar. That doesn't work on your iPhone, but you can still find out the address of a link (and even see a preview of the page) before tapping it. Hold your finger on the link for a few seconds. Safari then displays a pop-up screen showing the domain of the link and a preview of the linked page, as shown in

Figure 5.1. If the link looks legit, either tap Open to surf there in the current browser tab or tap Open in New Tab to start a fresh tab (see the section about opening and managing multiple browser tabs later in this chapter for more information). If you decide not to follow the link, tap an empty part of the screen.

- **Tap and hold to make a copy of a link address.** If you want to include a link address in another app, such as a note or an email message, you can copy it. Tap and hold your finger on the link for a few seconds, and Safari displays the pop-up screen shown in Figure 5.1. Tap Copy to place the link address into memory, switch to the other app, tap the cursor, and then tap Paste.
- **Quick access to common top-level domains.** A top-level domain (TLD) is the part of the domain name that comes after the last dot. For example, in wiley.com, the *.com* part is the TLD. You might think you have to type them the old-fashioned way. Nope! Tap and hold the period (.) key, and a pop-up appears with keys for .com, .net, .edu, and .org, and another for your current country TLD (such as .us for the United States). Slide your finger over to the one you want.

Domain of the linked page

5.1 Hold your finger on a link to see the domain, a preview of the page, and several link options.

Browsing Tips for Faster Surfing

If you're like me, the biggest problem you have with the web is that it's just so darned huge. We spend great big chunks of our day visiting sites and still never seem to get to everything on that day's To Surf list. The iPhone helps lessen (but, alas, not eliminate) this problem by allowing you to surf wherever Wi-Fi can be found (or just wherever if you only have a cellular connection). Even so, the faster and more efficient your iPhone surfing sessions are, the more sites you see. The touchscreen tips I covered earlier can help, and in this section, I take you through a few more useful tips for speedier surfing.

Opening and managing multiple browser tabs

When you're perusing web pages, what happens when you're on a page that you want to keep reading, but you also need to leap over to another page for something? You can open a second tab and load the other different page into it. Then, it's just a quick tap and flick to switch between the two tabs. You're not restricted to a meager two tabs either. Your iPhone lets you open up as many tabs as you need.

Note

Some web page links are configured to automatically open the page in a new window, so you might see a new tab being created when you tap a link. Also, if you add a Safari bookmark to your Home screen (as described in Chapter 2), tapping the icon opens the web page in a new Safari tab.

Here are the steps to follow to open and load multiple tabs:

1. **If you don't see the menu bar at the bottom of the Safari screen, tap the title bar that appears at the top of the screen, or swipe down on the screen.** Safari reveals its menu bar.
2. **Tap the Tabs button in the menu bar (see Figure 5.2).** Safari displays a thumbnail version of the current tab.

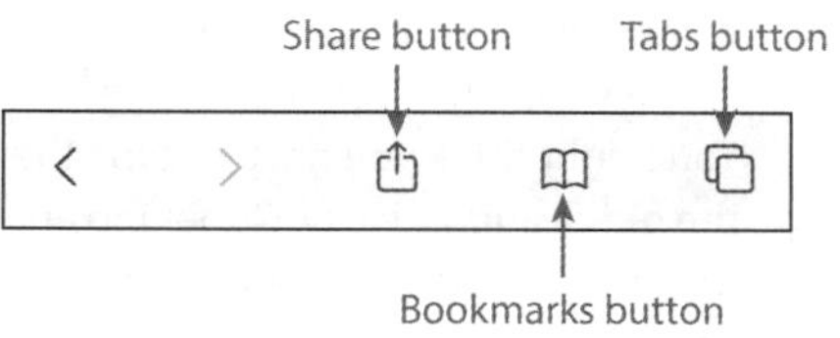

5.2 Tap the Tabs button to open a new tab.

Genius

To customize what you see in the New Tab screen, open the Settings app and then tap Safari. To hide the sites you've visited most often, tap the Frequently Visited Sites switch to Off. To specify a different collection of pages to appear as the Favorites, tap Favorites and then tap the folder you want to use. To add the current page to the Favorites list, tap Share (see Figure 5.2) and then tap Add to Favorites.

3. **Tap New Tab (the + button at the bottom of the screen; see Figure 5.3).** Safari opens a new tab and displays a list of favorite and frequently visited sites.
4. **Load a website into the new tab.** You can do this by tapping a favorite or frequent site, selecting a bookmark, entering an address, or whatever.
5. **Repeat Steps 1 to 4 to load as many tabs as you need.**

Once you have two or more tabs fired up, here are a couple of techniques you can use to impress your friends:

- **Switch to another tab.** Tap the Tabs button to get to the thumbnail view (see Figure 5.3). Flick up or down to bring the page into view, and then tap the page.
- **Delete a tab.** Tap the Tabs button to open the thumbnails, flick up or down to bring the page into view, and then tap the X in the upper-left corner of the thumbnail (or tap and drag the page off the left edge of the screen). Safari trashes the page without a whimper of protest.

5.3 Tap the Tabs button to see thumbnail versions of your open tabs.

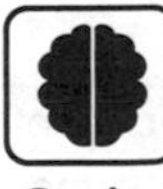

Genius

You can configure Safari to close old tabs automatically. Open the Settings app, tap Safari, and then tap Close Tabs. Tap the amount of time that a tab has been open after which you want Safari to close the tab for you: After One Day, After One Week, or After One Month.

Opening a tab in the background

When you tap and hold a link and then tap Open in New Tab, Safari creates a new tab, switches to that tab, and then loads the new page in the tab. That's often the behavior you want because it lets you check out the new tab right away. However, you might prefer to have Safari load the page in a new tab but without switching to that tab, which enables you to keep reading the current page.

Follow these steps to configure Safari to always open new tabs in the background:

1. **On the Home screen, tap Settings.** The Settings app slides in.
2. **Tap Safari.** Your iPhone displays the Safari screen.
3. **In the Tabs section, tap Open Links.** Your iPhone displays the Open Links screen.
4. **Tap In Background.**

With that done, when you now tap and hold a link, you see the Open in Background command (instead of Open in New Tab), which you can tap to open the page behind the scenes, as it were.

Viewing a page without distractions

Safari offers the Reader view feature, which removes all those extraneous page distractions — such as background colors or images that clash with the text; ads above, to the side of, and within the text; site features such as search boxes, feed links, and content lists; and those ubiquitous icons for sharing the article on social media — that just get in the way of your reading pleasure. Instead of a cacophony of text, icons, and images, you see pure, simple, large-enough-to-be-easily-read text.

How do you arrive at this blissful state? By tapping the View icon, which appears on the left side of the address bar, as pointed out in Figure 5.4, and then tapping Show Reader View. Safari instantly transforms the page, and you see something similar to the page shown in Figure 5.5 (which is the Reader view version of the page shown in Figure 5.4). To go back to the regular view, tap View and then tap Hide Reader View.

Requesting a web site's desktop version

Many web sites recognize that you're surfing iPhone-style and display a "mobile" version of the site. This version is usually easier to read and navigate, but that ease almost always comes at the cost of having access to fewer site features. If a site isn't displaying the feature you

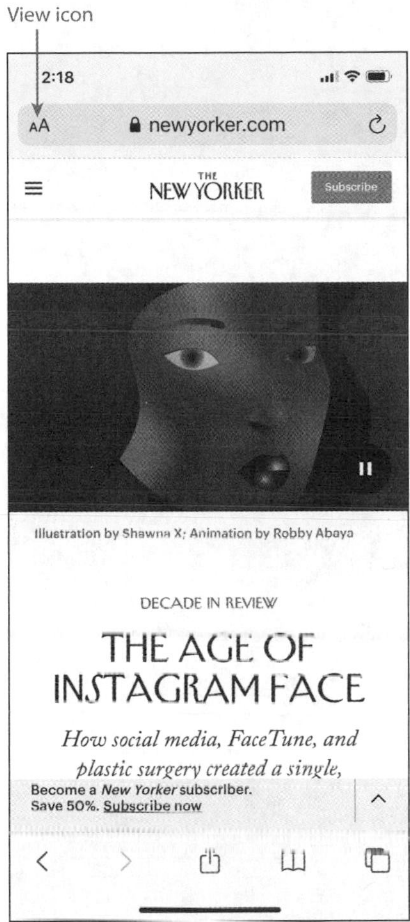

5.4 Today's web pages are all too often festooned with ads, icons, and other bric-a-brac.

want, you can request the site's "desktop" version (that is, the full version that you'd see if you were using a desktop computer). To try this, tap View (pointed out in Figure 5.4) and then tap Request Desktop Website. To go back, tap View and then tap Request Mobile Website.

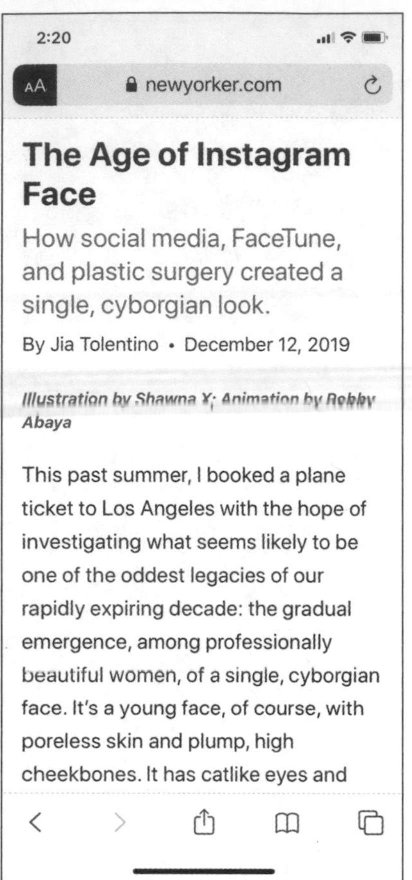

2:20

AA newyorker.com

The Age of Instagram Face

How social media, FaceTune, and plastic surgery created a single, cyborgian look.

By Jia Tolentino • December 12, 2019

Illustration by Shawna X; Animation by Robby Abaya

This past summer, I booked a plane ticket to Los Angeles with the hope of investigating what seems likely to be one of the oddest legacies of our rapidly expiring decade: the gradual emergence, among professionally beautiful women, of a single, cyborgian face. It's a young face, of course, with poreless skin and plump, high cheekbones. It has catlike eyes and

5.5 The Reader view version of a web page is a simple and easy-to-read text affair.

Genius

If you want Safari to request the desktop version of all the web sites you visit, open the Settings app, tap Safari, tap Request Desktop Website, and then tap the All Websites switch to On.

Saving sites as bookmarks

Although you've seen that the Safari browser on your iPhone offers a few tricks to ease the pain of typing web page addresses, it's still slower and quite a bit more cumbersome than a full-size, physical keyboard (which lets even inexpert typists rattle off addresses lickety-split). That's all the more reason that you should embrace bookmarks with all your heart. After all, a bookmark lets you jump to a web page with precisely no typing — just a tap or three and you're there. Here are the steps to follow:

1. **On the iPhone, use Safari to navigate to the site you want to save.**
2. **Display the menu bar (by tapping the web page title bar or swiping down on the screen) and then tap the Share button in the menu bar.** This is the button with the arrow in the middle of the Safari menu bar (pointed out earlier in Figure 5.2).
3. **Tap Add Bookmark.** This opens the Add Bookmark screen.
4. **Tap in the top box and enter a name for the site that helps you remember it.** This name is what you see when you scroll through your bookmarks.
5. **Tap Location.** This displays a list of your bookmark folders.
6. **Tap the folder you want to use to store the bookmark.** Safari returns you to the Add Bookmark screen.
7. **Tap Save.** Safari saves the bookmark.

Managing your bookmarks

Once you have a few bookmarks stashed away in the Bookmarks list, you may need to perform a few housekeeping chores from time to time, including changing a bookmark's name, address, or folder; reordering bookmarks or folders; or getting rid of bookmarks that have worn out their welcome.

Before you can do any of this, you need to get the Bookmarks list into Edit mode by following these steps:

1. **Display the menu bar (by tapping the web page title bar or swiping down on the screen) and then tap the Bookmarks button in the menu bar.** I pointed out this button earlier in Figure 5.2. Safari opens the Bookmarks list.
2. **Tap the Bookmarks tab.**

3. **If the bookmark you want to mess with is located in a particular folder, tap to open that folder.** For example, if you've synced with Safari, then you should have a folder named Bookmarks Bar that includes all the bookmarks and folders that you've added to the Bookmarks Bar in your desktop version of Safari.
4. **Tap Edit.** Your iPhone switches the Bookmarks list to Edit mode. With Edit mode on the go, you're free to toil away at your bookmarks. Here are the techniques to master:
   - **Edit bookmark info.** Tap the bookmark to fire up the Edit Bookmark screen. From here, you can edit the bookmark name, address, or folder. Tap Done when you're ready to move on.
   - **Change the bookmark order.** Use the Drag icon on the right to tap and drag a bookmark to a new position in the list. Ideally, you should move your favorite bookmarks near the top of the list for easiest access.
   - **Add a bookmark folder.** Tap New Folder to launch the Edit Folder screen; then tap a folder title and select a location. Feel free to use bookmark folders at will because they're a great way to keep your bookmarks neat and tidy (if you're into that kind of thing).
   - **Delete a bookmark.** No use for a particular bookmark? No problem. Tap the Delete button — the minus (–) sign to the left of the bookmark — and then tap the Delete button that appears.

When the dust settles and your bookmark chores are done for the day, tap Done to get out of Edit mode and then tap Done to exit the Bookmarks screen.

Saving a page to read later

Safari offers a feature called the Reading List that is, as the name implies, a simple list of things to read. When you don't have time to read something now, add it to your Reading List and you can read it at your leisure.

There are a couple of techniques you can use to add a page to your Reading List:

- Use Safari to navigate to the page that you want to read later, tap the Share button, and then tap Add to Reading List. If Safari asks whether you want to save articles automatically for offline reading, tap Save Automatically.
- Tap and hold a link for the page that you want to read later and then tap Add to Reading List.

When you're settled into your favorite easy chair and have the time (finally!) to read, open Safari, tap the Bookmarks button, and then tap the Reading List tab (the eyeglasses icon). Safari displays all the items you've added to the list, and you just tap the article you want to read. To make the list a bit easier to manage, tap Show Unread to see just the pages you haven't yet perused.

Retracing your steps with the handy History list

Bookmarking a web site is a good idea if that site contains interesting or fun content that you want to revisit in the future. Unfortunately, you may have run into Murphy's Web Browsing Law: A cool site that you forget to bookmark is never found again. Fortunately, your iPhone has your back. As you navigate the nooks and crannies of the web, iPhone keeps track of where you go, storing the name and address of each page in the History list. The limited memory on iPhone means that it can't store tons of sites, but it might have the one you're looking for. Here's how to use it:

1. **Display the menu bar (by tapping the web page title bar or swiping down on the screen) and then tap the Bookmarks button.** Safari opens the Bookmarks list.
2. **Tap the History tab (the clock icon).** Safari opens the History screen, which shows the sites you've visited today at the top, followed by a list of previous surfing dates.
3. **If you visited the site you're looking for on a previous day, tap that day.** Safari displays a list of only the sites you visited on that day.
4. **Tap the site you want to revisit.** Safari loads it.

Filling in Online Forms

Many web pages include forms where you fill in some data and submit it, which sends the data off to some server for processing. Filling in these forms in your Safari browser is mostly straightforward:

- **Text box.** Tap inside the text box to display the touchscreen keyboard, tap out your text, and then tap Done.
- **Text area.** Tap inside the text area and then use the keyboard to tap your text. Most text areas allow multiline entries, so you can tap Return to start a new line. When you finish, tap Done.

- **Check box.** Tap the check box to toggle the check mark on and off.
- **Radio button.** Tap the radio button to activate it.
- **Command button.** Tap the button to make it do its thing (usually submit the form).

Many online forms consist of a bunch of text boxes. If the idea of performing the tap-type-Done cycle over and over isn't appealing to you, fear not. The Safari browser on your iPhone offers an easier method:

1. **Tap inside the first text box.** The keyboard appears.
2. **Tap to type the text you want to submit.** Above the keyboard, notice the Previous and Next buttons, as shown in Figure 5.6.
3. **Tap Next to move to the next text box.** If you need to return to a text box, tap Previous instead.
4. **Repeat Steps 2 and 3 to fill in the text boxes.**
5. **Tap Done.** Safari returns you to the page.

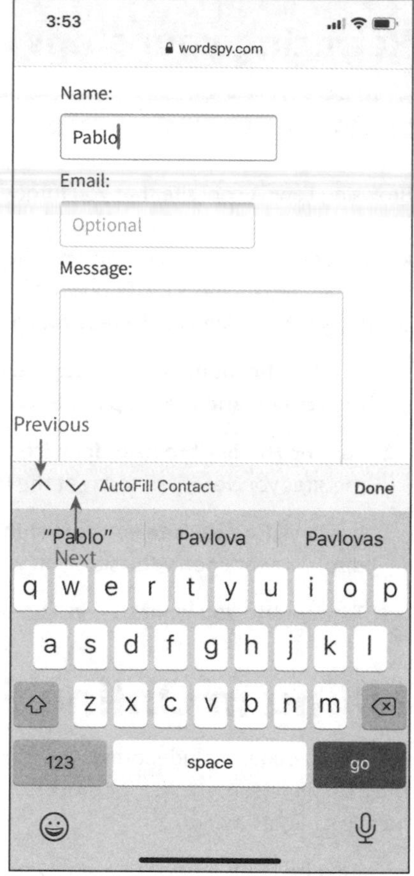

5.6 If the form contains multiple text boxes, you can use the Previous and Next buttons to navigate them.

I haven't yet talked about selection lists, and that's because the browser on your iPhone handles them in an interesting way. When you tap a list, Safari displays the list items in a picker, as shown in Figure 5.7. Tap the item you want to select. As with text boxes, if the form has multiple lists, you see the Previous and Next buttons, which you can tap to navigate from one list to another. After you make all your selections, tap Done to return to the page.

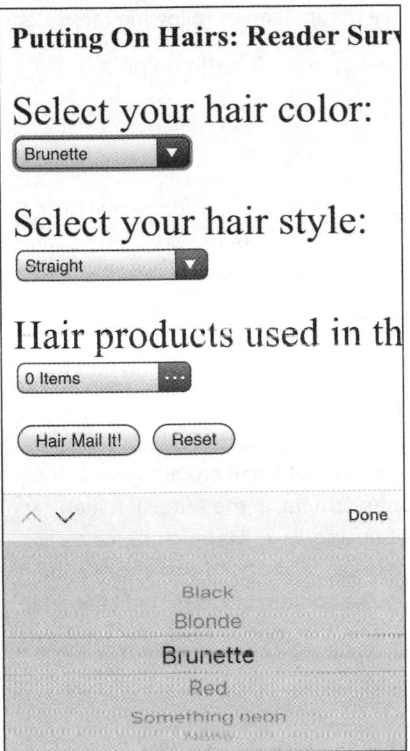

5.7 Tap a list to see its items in a separate box for easier selection.

Turning on AutoFill for faster form input

The Safari browser on your iPhone makes it relatively easy to fill in online forms, but it can still be slow going, particularly if you have to do a lot of typing. To help make forms less of a chore, Safari supports a welcome feature called AutoFill. Just as with the desktop version of Safari (or just about any other mainstream browser), AutoFill remembers the data you enter into forms and then enables you to fill in similar forms with a simple tap of a button.

To take advantage of this nifty feature, you first have to turn it on by following these steps:

1. **In the Home screen, tap Settings.** Your iPhone opens the Settings app.
2. **Tap Safari.** The Safari screen appears.
3. **Tap AutoFill to open the AutoFill screen.**
4. **Tap the Use Contact Info switch to On.** This tells Safari to use your item in the Contacts app to grab data for a form. For example, if a form requires your name, Safari uses your contact name. Safari displays the All Contacts screen.
5. **Tap My Info and then tap your name in the Contacts list.**
6. **If you want Safari to remember the credit card data you enter when making online purchases, tap the Credit Cards switch to On.**

Genius

You could add your credit card data by hand, but Safari enables you to enter the data automatically using the iPhone's camera. In the AutoFill screen, tap Saved Credit Cards; verify your identity using Face ID, Touch ID, or a passcode (you really should be using one of these safety features if you're adding credit cards to your iPhone; see Chapter 2); and then tap Add Credit Card. Tap Use Camera, position the credit card within the camera field, and then wait until the card info is recognized.

Now when you visit an online form and access any text field in the form, the AutoFill Contact button becomes enabled. Tap AutoFill Contact to fill in those portions of the form that correspond with your contact data, as shown in Figure 5.8. Notice that the fields Safari was able to automatically fill in appear with a colored background (First Name and Last Name, in this case).

5.8 Tap the AutoFill button to fill in form fields with your contact data.

Saving web site login passwords

In the previous section, I discuss using the AutoFill feature to automatically enter form data, such as your name. You can also configure AutoFill to remember web site passwords. Follow these steps to activate this feature:

1. **In the Home screen, tap Settings.** iOS opens the Settings app.
2. **Tap Passwords.** iOS prompts you to identify yourself using Face ID, Touch ID, or a passcode.
3. **Verify your identity.** The Passwords screen appears.
4. **Tap the AutoFill Passwords switch to On.**

Once you enable the AutoFill Passwords option, each time you fill in a password to log in to a site, Safari displays the dialog shown in Figure 5.9. It asks if you want to remember the login data and gives you three choices:

- **Save Password.** Tap this button to have Safari remember your username and password.
- **Never for This Website.** Tap this button to tell Safari not to remember the username and password and to never again prompt you to save the login data.
- **Not Now.** Tap this button to tell Safari not to remember the username and password this time, but to prompt you again next time you log in to this site.

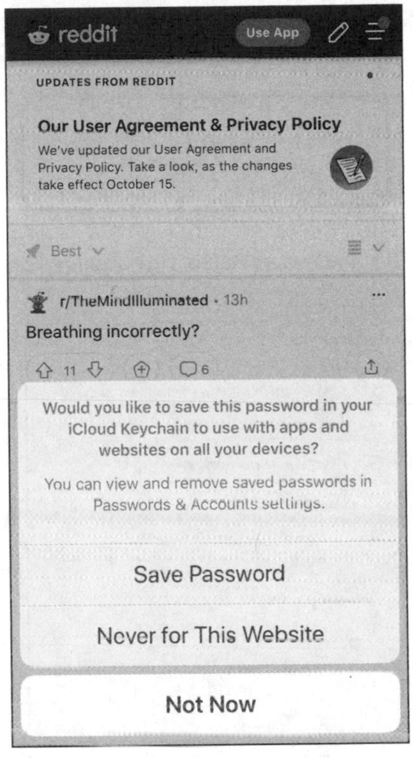

5.9 If you configured Safari to remember usernames and passwords, you see this dialog when you log in to a site.

Genius

If you tap Save Password but then change your mind, you can remove the saved password from your iPhone. Tap Settings, tap Passwords, and then verify your identity (via Face ID, Touch ID, or a passcode) to see a list of the sites with saved passwords. Swipe left on the site you want to remove and then tap the Delete button that appears.

Note

Your iPhone is cautious about this password stuff, so it doesn't offer to save all the passwords you enter. In particular, if the login form is part of a secure site, then your iPhone doesn't ask if you want to save the password. This means you won't be tempted to store the password for your online bank, corporate web site, or any other site that requires secure access.

To use a saved password, surf to the site's login page and tap one of the login fields, such as the username or password field. Safari displays a prompt similar to the one shown at the bottom of the screen in Figure 5.10. Either tap the suggested login or tap Keychain (pointed out in Figure 5.10) to see a list of saved passwords for the site (yes, you can have more than one saved password for a site) and then tap the login you want to use. Safari fills in the login data, so all you have to do is tap Log In (or Sign In, or whatever).

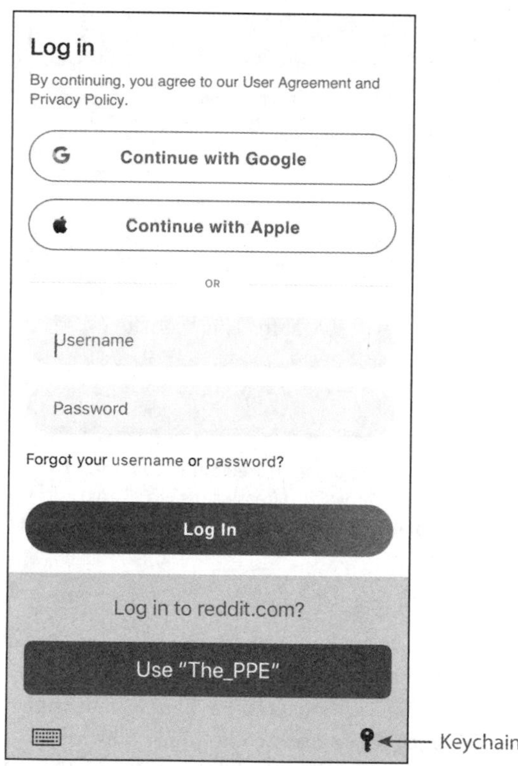

5.10 If you've saved the login data for a site, Safari asks if it can automatically fill in that data the next time you log in to the site.

Adding web site passwords manually

For saving passwords on your iPhone, it's easiest just to fill in your username and password online and then let Safari save the logon data for you. However, if the site or your Internet connection is temporarily unavailable, you can still enter a web site's password by hand. You might also want to add a second (or third) set of login data to an existing site, and that's usually easiest to do manually. Here's how:

1. **Tap Settings to display the Settings app.**
2. **Tap Passwords and then verify your identity using Face ID, Touch ID, or a passcode.** The Passwords screen appears.
3. **Tap Add Password (+) at the top of the screen.** The Add Password screen appears.
4. **Fill in the web site's address, your username, and your password.** The password appears in regular text instead of the usual dots, so make sure no one's peeking over your shoulder as you do this.
5. **Tap Done.** Settings saves the login data for the site.

Getting More Out of Safari on Your iPhone

You've seen a lot of great Safari tips and techniques so far in this chapter, but I hope you're up for even more, because you've got a ways to go. In the rest of this chapter, you learn such useful techniques as maintaining your privacy, changing the default search engine, configuring the Safari security options, and searching a web page.

Maintaining your privacy by deleting the History list

The History list of sites you've recently surfed on your iPhone is a great feature when you need it, and it's an innocuous feature when you don't. However, there are times when the History list is just plain uncool. For example, if you visit a private corporate site, a financial site, or any other site you wouldn't want others to see, the History list might betray you.

And sometimes unsavory sites can end up in your History list by accident. For example, you might tap a legitimate-looking link in a web page or email message, only to end up in some dark, dank net neighborhood. Of course, you hightail it out of there right away with a quick tap of the Back button, but that nasty site is now lurking in your history.

Whether you've got sites on the History list that you wouldn't want anyone to see or you just find the idea of your iPhone tracking your movements on the web to be a bit sinister, follow these steps to wipe out the History list:

1. **In Safari, display the menu bar (by tapping the web page title bar or swiping down on the screen) and then tap the Bookmarks button.** Safari opens the Bookmarks list.
2. **Tap the History tab (the clock icon).** Safari opens the History screen.
3. **Tap Clear.** Safari asks how much of your history you want to clear.
4. **Tap a time period: The Last Hour, Today, Today and Yesterday, or All Time.** Safari deletes every site from the History list for that time period.

Genius

One good thing about your web site history is that Safari can use it (as well as your bookmarks) to analyze each page you view and determine the most likely link you'll tap — the so-called *top hit* — and preload that link. If you do tap that link, the page loads lickety-split. If you're comfortable having Safari send your history and bookmarks to Apple, you can activate this feature. Tap Settings, tap Safari, and then tap the Preload Top Hit switch to On.

Deleting website data

As you wander around the web, Safari gathers and saves bits of information for each site. For example, it stores some site text and images so that it can display the page faster if you revisit the site in the near future. Similarly, if you activated AutoFill for names and passwords, Safari stores that data on your iPhone. Finally, most major sites store small text files called *cookies* on your iPhone that save information for things like site preferences and shopping carts.

Storing all this data on your iPhone is generally a good thing because it can speed up your surfing. However, it's not always a safe or private thing. For example, if you elect to have Safari save a site password, you might change your mind later, particularly if you share your iPhone with other people. Similarly, cookies can sometimes be used to track your activities online, so they're not always benign.

Here are the steps to follow to delete data for individual web sites:

1. **On the Home screen, tap Settings.** Your iPhone opens the Settings app.
2. **Tap Safari.** The Safari screen appears.
3. **At the bottom of the screen, tap Advanced.** The Advanced screen appears.

4. **Tap Website Data.** Safari displays a list of the recent sites for which it has stored data, as well as the size of that data.
5. **If you don't see the site you want to remove, tap Show All Sites at the bottom of the list.**
6. **Tap Edit.**
7. **Tap the red Delete icon to the left of the site you want to clear.**
8. **Tap the Delete button that appears to the right of the site's data size value.** Safari removes the site's data.

Genius

Rather than deleting web site data one site at a time, you might want to clean house by deleting *all* the web site data currently stored by Safari. It's a drastic move, but it can come in handy if you're selling your phone or allowing someone else to use it for a while. In the Website Data screen, tap Remove All Website Data. When your iPhone asks you to confirm, tap Remove Now.

Browsing privately

If you find yourself constantly deleting your browsing history or web site data, you can save yourself a bit of time by configuring Safari to do this automatically. This is called *private browsing*, and it means that Safari doesn't save any data as you browse. Specifically, it doesn't save the following:

- Sites aren't added to the history (although the Back and Forward buttons still work for navigating sites that you've visited in the current session).
- Web page text and images aren't saved.
- Search text isn't saved with the search box.
- Web site cookies aren't used.
- AutoFill passwords aren't saved.

To activate private browsing, follow these steps:

1. **In Safari, display the menu bar (by tapping the web page title bar or swiping down on the screen) and then tap the Tabs button.**
2. **Tap Private in the lower-left corner of the screen.** Safari creates a separate set of tabs for private browsing.
3. **Tap Add Tab (+).** Safari creates a new private tab.

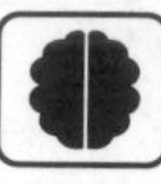

Genius

Another way Safari might compromise your online privacy is by displaying suggestions as you enter search text into the address bar. If someone is looking over your shoulder or simply borrows your iPhone for a quick search, she might see these suggestions. To turn them off, open the Settings app, tap Safari, and then tap both the Search Engine Suggestions switch and the Safari Suggestions switch to Off.

Changing the default search engine

Google is the default search engine on your iPhone. Almost everyone uses Google, of course, but if you have something against it, you can switch and use a different search engine. Here's how:

1. **In the Home screen, tap Settings.** Your iPhone opens the Settings app.
2. **Tap Safari.** The Safari screen appears.
3. **Tap Search Engine.** Your iPhone opens the Search Engine screen.
4. **Tap the search engine you want to use.** You have four choices: Google, Yahoo!, Bing, or DuckDuckGo.

Searching web page text

When you're perusing a page on the web, it's not unusual to be looking for specific information. In those situations, rather than reading through the entire page to find the info you seek, it would be a lot easier to search for the data. You can easily do this in the desktop version of Safari or any other computer browser, but, at first glance, the Safari app doesn't seem to have a Find feature anywhere. It's there all right, but you need to know where to look:

1. **Use Safari to navigate to the web page that contains the information you seek.**
2. **Display the menu bar (by tapping the web page title bar or swiping down on the screen) and then tap the Share icon.**
3. **Tap Find on Page.** Safari displays the search text box.
4. **Type the search text you want to use.** Safari highlights the first instance of the search term, as shown in Figure 5.11.

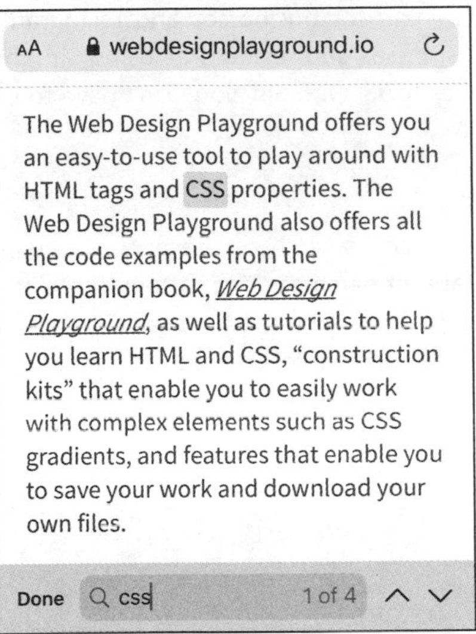

5.11 Safari highlights the first instance of the search term that appears on the current web page.

5. **Tap the down-pointing arrow to cycle forward through the instances of the search term that appear on the page.** Note that you can also cycle backward through the results by tapping the up-pointing arrow. Also, when you tap the down-pointing arrow after the last result appears, Safari returns you to the first result.

6. **When you're finished with the search, tap Done.**

Searching the web with Siri voice commands

You can use Safari to type search queries either directly into the search box or by navigating to a search engine site. However, typing suddenly seems like such a quaint pastime thanks to the voice-recognition prowess of the Siri app. So why type a search query when you can just tell Siri what you're looking for? If you agree, here are some general tips for web searching with Siri:

- **Searching the entire web.** Say "Search the web for *topic*," where *topic* is your search criteria.
- **Searching Wikipedia.** Say "Search Wikipedia for *topic*," where *topic* is the subject you want to look up.
- **Searching with a particular search engine.** Say "Use *Engine* to search for *topic*," where *Engine* is the name of the search engine, such as Google or Bing, and *topic* is your search criteria.

Siri also understands commands related to searching for businesses and restaurants through its partnership with Yelp. To look for businesses and restaurants using Siri, the general syntax to use is the following (although, as usual with Siri, you don't have to be too rigid about this):

"Find (or Look for) *something somewhere.*"

Here, the *something* part can be the name of a business (such as "Starbucks"), a type of business (such as "gas station"), a type of restaurant (such as "Thai restaurants"), or a generic product (such as "coffee"). The *somewhere* part can be something relative to your current location (such as "around here" or "near me" or "within walking distance") or a specific location (such as "in Indianapolis" or "in Broad Ripple"). Here are some examples:

- "Find a gas station within walking distance."
- "Look for pizza restaurants in Indianapolis."
- "Find coffee around here."
- "Look for a grocery store near me."

Note, too, that if you add a qualifier such as "good" or "best" before the *something* portion of the command, Siri returns the results organized by their Yelp rating.

Sharing a link via AirDrop

Here's an all-too-common scenario in this digital, mobile age: You're out with friends or colleagues, you look up something on your iPhone, and you find a page that one of your peeps wants to check out. How do you get the page address from your iPhone to her device? iOS uses AirDrop, a Bluetooth service that lets two nearby devices — specifically, an iPhone, an iPad, or a Mac running OS X Yosemite or later — exchange a link wirelessly. Here's how it works:

1. **Use Safari to navigate to the web page you want to share.**
2. **Display the menu bar (by tapping the web page title bar or swiping down on the screen) and then tap the Share icon.**
3. **Tap AirDrop.** The AirDrop screen appears and shows an icon for each nearby device.
4. **Tap the icon for the person with whom you want to share the link.** The other person sees a confirmation dialog. When she taps Accept, her version of Safari (or her default browser) loads and displays the page. Pie-easy!

How Do I Maximize iPhone Email?

Email has been called the "killer app" of the Internet, and it certainly deserves that title. Yes, chat and instant messaging are popular; social networks such as Facebook, Twitter, and Instagram get a lot of press; and blogging sites appeal to a certain type of person. However, while not everyone uses these services, it's safe to say that almost everyone uses email. You probably use email all day, particularly when you're on the go with your iPhone in tow, so learning a few useful and efficient email techniques can make your day a bit easier and save you time for more important pursuits.

Managing Your iPhone Email Accounts

Your iPhone comes with the Mail app, which is a slimmed-down version of the Mail application that's the default email program on macOS. Mail on the iPhone may be smaller than its OS X cousin, but that doesn't mean it's a lightweight — far from it. It has a few features and settings that make it ideal for your traveling email show. First, however, you have to set up your iPhone with one or more email accounts.

Adding an account by hand

The Mail application on your iPhone is most useful when it's set up to use an email account that you also use on your computer. That way, when you're on the road or out on the town, you can check your messages and rest assured that you won't miss anything important (or even anything unimportant, for that matter).

However, you might also prefer to have an email account that's for iPhone only. For example, if you sign up for an iPhone newsletter, you might prefer to have those messages sent to only your iPhone. That's a darn good idea, but it means that you have to set up the account on the iPhone itself, which, as you'll soon see, requires a fair amount of tapping.

How you create an account on your iPhone with the sweat of your own brow depends on the type of account you have. First, there are the six email services that your iPhone recognizes:

- **iCloud.** This is the Apple web-based email service (that also comes with applications for calendars, contacts, and more).
- **Microsoft Exchange.** Your iPhone supports accounts on Exchange servers, which are common in large organizations like corporations or schools. Exchange uses a central server to store messages, and you usually work with your messages on the server, not your iPhone. However, one of the great features in the iPhone is support for Exchange ActiveSync, which automatically keeps your phone and your account on the server synchronized.
- **Google.** This refers to Gmail, a web-based email service run by Google.
- **Yahoo!** This is a web-based email service run by Yahoo!.

- **AOL.** This is a web-based email service run by AOL.
- **Outlook.com.** This is a web-based email service run by Microsoft.

Your iPhone knows how to connect to these services, so to set up any of these email accounts you only need to know the address and the account password.

Otherwise, your iPhone Mail app supports the following email account types:

- **POP (Post Office Protocol).** This is the most popular type of account. Its main characteristic for your purposes is that incoming messages are stored only temporarily on the provider's mail server. When you connect to the server, the messages are downloaded to your iPhone and removed from the server. In other words, your messages (including copies of messages you send) are stored locally on your iPhone. The advantage here is that you don't need to be online to read your email. Once it's downloaded to your iPhone, you can read it or delete it at your leisure.
- **IMAP (Internet Message Access Protocol).** This type of account is most often used with web-based email services. It's the opposite of POP (sort of) because all your incoming messages, as well as copies of messages you send, remain on the server. In this case, when Mail works with an IMAP account, it connects to the server and works with the messages on the server, not on your iPhone (although it looks like you're working with the messages locally). The advantage here is that you can access the messages from multiple devices and multiple locations, but you must be connected to the Internet to work with your messages.

Your network administrator or your email service provider can let you know what type of email account you have. Your administrator or provider can also give you the information you need to set up the account. This includes your email address, the username and password you use to check for new messages (and perhaps also the security information you need to specify to send messages), the host name of the incoming mail server (typically something like mail.*provider*.com, where *provider*.com is the domain name of the provider), and the host name of the outgoing mail server (typically either mail.*provider*.com or smtp.*provider*.com).

With your account information ready, follow these steps to forge a new account:

1. **On the Home screen, tap Settings.** Your iPhone opens the Settings app.
2. **Tap Mail.** iOS displays the Mail settings.
3. **Tap Accounts.** The Accounts screen appears.

4. **Tap Add Account.** This opens the Add Account screen, as shown in Figure 6.1.
5. **You have two ways to proceed:**
   - **If you're adding an account for iCloud, Exchange, Google, Yahoo!, AOL, or Outlook.com, tap the corresponding logo.** In the account information screen that appears, enter your name, your email address, a password, and an account description. Tap Next, make sure the Mail switch is set to On, tap Save, and you're done!
   - **If you're adding another account type, tap Other and continue with Step 5.**
6. **Tap Add Mail Account to open the New Account screen.**
7. **Use the Name, Email, and Description text boxes to enter the corresponding account information, and then tap Next.**
8. **Tap the type of account you're adding: IMAP or POP.**
9. **In the Incoming Mail Server section, use the Host Name text box to enter the host name of your provider's incoming mail server, as well as your username and password.**
10. **In the Outgoing Mail Server (SMTP) section, use the Host Name text box to enter the host name of your provider's outgoing (SMTP) mail server.** If your provider requires a username and password to send messages, enter those as well.
11. **Tap Save.** Your iPhone verifies the account info and then returns you to the Mail settings screen with the account added to the Accounts list.

6.1 Use the Add Account screen to choose the type of email account you want to add.

Specifying the default account

If you've added two or more email accounts to your iPhone, Mail specifies one of them as the default account. This means that Mail uses this account when you send a new message, when you reply to a message, and when you forward a message. The default account is usually the first account you add to your iPhone. However, you can change this by following these steps:

1. **On the Home screen, tap Settings.** The Settings app appears.
2. **Tap Mail.** Your iPhone displays the Mail settings.
3. **At the bottom of the Composing section, tap Default Account.** This opens the Default Account screen, which displays a list of your accounts. The current default account is shown with a check mark beside it.
4. **Tap the account you want to use as the default.** Your iPhone places a check mark beside the account.

Temporarily disabling an account

The Mail app checks for new messages at a regular interval. If you have several accounts configured in Mail, this incessant checking can put quite a strain on your iPhone battery. To ease up on the juice, you can disable an account temporarily to prevent Mail from checking it for new messages. Here's how:

1. **On the Home screen, tap Settings.** Your iPhone displays the Settings app.
2. **Tap Mail.** iOS displays the Mail settings.
3. **Tap Accounts.** The Accounts screen appears.
4. **Tap the account you want to disable.** Your iPhone displays the account's settings.
5. **Depending on the type of account, use one of the following techniques to temporarily disable the account:**
   - **For an iCloud, Exchange, Google, Yahoo!, AOL, Outlook.com, or IMAP account, tap the Mail switch to Off, as shown in Figure 6.2.** If the account syncs other types of data, such as contacts and calendars, you can also turn off those switches, if you want.
   - **For a POP account, tap the Account switch to Off.**

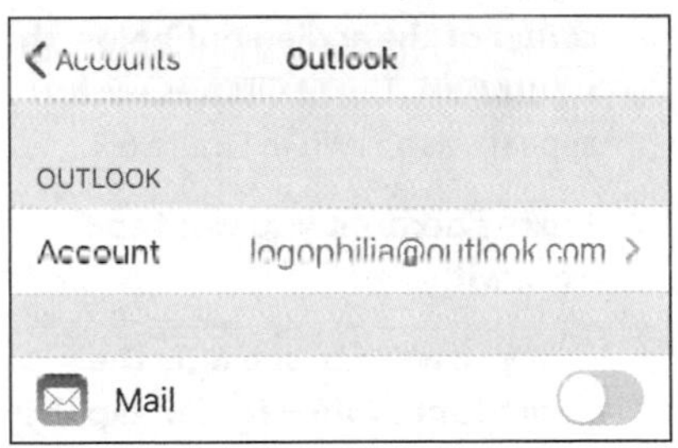

6.2 For an iCloud, Exchange, Google, Yahoo!, AOL, Outlook.com, or IMAP account, tap the Mail switch to Off.

When you're ready to work with the account again, repeat these steps to turn the Mail switch or the Account switch back to On.

Deleting an account

If an email account has grown tiresome and boring (or you just don't use it anymore), you should delete it to save storage space, speed up sync times, and save battery power. Follow these steps:

1. **On the Home screen, tap Settings.** The Settings app appears.
2. **Tap Mail.** iOS displays the Mail settings.
3. **Tap Accounts.** The Accounts screen appears.
4. **Tap the account you want to delete.** This opens the account's settings.
5. **At the bottom of the screen, tap Delete Account.** Your iPhone asks you to confirm.
6. **Tap Delete Account.** Your iPhone returns you to the Mail settings screen, and the account no longer graces the Accounts list.

Switching to another account

When you open the Mail app, you usually see the Inbox folder of your default account. If you have multiple accounts set up on your iPhone and you want to see what's going on with a different account, follow these steps to make the switch:

1. **On the Home screen, tap Mail to open the Mail app.**
2. **Tap the Back button (the left-pointing arrow that appears in the top-left corner of the screen but below the status bar).** The Mailboxes screen appears, as shown in Figure 6.3.
3. **Tap the account you want to work with:**
   - **If you want to see only the account's Inbox folder, tap the account name in the top part of the Mailboxes screen (under the All Inboxes folder).**
   - **If you want to see all the account's available folders, tap the account name in the Accounts section of**

6.3 Use the Mailboxes screen to choose another email account.

the Mailboxes screen. Mail displays a list of the account's folders, and you then tap the folder you want to work with.

Genius

You can customize the folders you see in the Mailboxes screen. For example, you can display the Unread folder to see all your unread messages, or you can display the Attachments folder to see all your messages that have one or more files attached. In the Mailboxes screen, tap Edit, tap to activate each folder you want to see (or deactivate each folder you don't want to see), and then tap Done.

Configuring Email Accounts

Setting up an email account on your iPhone is one thing, but making that account do useful things — or sometimes, anything at all — is quite another. The next few sections take you through a few useful settings that help you to get more out of email and to troubleshoot email problems.

Managing multiple devices by leaving messages on the server

In today's increasingly mobile world, it's not unusual to find you need to check the same email account from multiple devices. For example, you might want to check your business account not only using your work computer but also using your home computer, or using your iPhone while commuting or traveling.

If you need to check email on multiple devices, you can take advantage of how POP email messages are delivered over the Internet. When someone sends you a message, it doesn't come directly to your computer. Instead, it goes to the server that your Internet service provider (or your company) has set up to handle incoming messages. When you ask Apple Mail to check for new messages, it communicates with the POP server to see whether any messages are waiting in your account. If so, Mail downloads those messages to your computer and then instructs the server to delete the copies of the messages stored on the server.

The trick, then, is to configure Mail so that it leaves copies of the messages on the POP server after you download them. That way, the messages are still available when you check messages using another device. Fortunately, the intuitive folks who designed the version of Mail on your iPhone must have understood this, because the program automatically sets up POP accounts to do just that. Specifically, after you download any messages from the POP server to your iPhone, Mail leaves the messages on the server.

Here's a good overall strategy that ensures you can download messages on all your devices, but prevents messages from piling up on the server:

- Let your main computer be the one that controls deleting the messages from the server. In OS X, the default setting in Mail is to delete messages from the server after one week, and that's fine.
- Set up all your other devices — particularly your iPhone — to not delete messages from the server.

It's a good idea to check your iPhone POP accounts to ensure they're not deleting messages from the server. To do that or to use a different setting — such as deleting messages after a week or when you delete them from your Inbox — follow these steps:

1. **On the Home screen, tap Settings.** The Settings app appears.
2. **Tap Mail.** iOS displays the Mail settings.
3. **Tap Accounts.** The Accounts screen appears.
4. **Tap the POP account you want to configure.** The account's Settings screen appears.
5. **Near the bottom of the screen, tap Advanced.** Your iPhone displays the Advanced screen.
6. **Tap Delete from Server.** The Delete from Server screen appears.
7. **Tap Never.** If you prefer that your iPhone delete messages from the server automatically, tap either Seven days or When Removed from Inbox.

Fixing outgoing email problems by using a different server port

For security reasons, some Internet service providers (ISPs) insist that all their customers' outgoing mail must be routed through the ISP's Simple Mail Transport Protocol (SMTP) server. This usually isn't a big deal if you're using an email account maintained by the ISP, but it can lead to the following problems if you are using an account provided by a third party (such as your web site host):

- Your ISP might block messages sent using the third-party account because it thinks you're trying to relay the message through the ISP's server (a technique often used by spammers).
- You might incur extra charges if your ISP allows only a certain amount of SMTP bandwidth per month or a certain number of sent messages, whereas the third-party account offers higher limits or no restrictions at all.

- You might have performance problems, with the ISP taking much longer to route messages than the third-party host.
- You might think you can solve the problem by specifying that the third-party host's outgoing mail is sent by default through port 25. When you use this port, the outgoing mail goes through the ISP's SMTP server.

To work around the problem, many third-party hosts offer access to their SMTP server via a port other than the standard port 25. For example, the iCloud SMTP server (smtp.icloud.com) also accepts connections on ports 465 and 587. Here's how to configure an email account to use a nonstandard SMTP port:

1. **On the Home screen, tap Settings.** You see the Settings app.
2. **Tap Mail.** iOS displays the Mail settings.
3. **Tap Accounts.** The Accounts screen appears.
4. **Tap the POP account you want to configure.** The account's Settings screen appears.
5. **Near the bottom of the screen, tap SMTP.** Your iPhone displays the SMTP screen.
6. **In the Primary Server section, tap the server.** Your iPhone displays the server settings.
7. **In the Outgoing Mail Server section, tap Server Port and then type the port number.**

Configuring authentication for outgoing mail

Because spam is such a big problem these days, many ISPs now require SMTP authentication for outgoing mail, which means that you must log on to the SMTP server to confirm that you're the person sending the mail (as opposed to some spammer spoofing your address). If your ISP requires authentication on outgoing messages, you need to configure your email account to provide the proper credentials.

If you're not too sure about any of this, check with your ISP. If that doesn't work out, by far the most common type of authentication is to specify a username and password (this happens behind the scenes when you send messages). Follow these steps to configure your iPhone email account with this kind of authentication:

1. **On the Home screen, tap Settings.** Your iPhone displays the Settings app.
2. **Tap Mail.** iOS displays the Mail settings.
3. **Tap Accounts.** The Accounts screen appears.

4. **Tap the POP account you want to configure.** The account's Settings screen appears.
5. **Near the bottom of the screen, tap SMTP.** Your iPhone displays the SMTP screen.
6. **In the Primary Server section, tap the server.** Your iPhone displays the server's Settings screen.
7. **In the Outgoing Mail Server section, tap Authentication.** Your iPhone displays the Authentication screen.
8. **Tap Password.**
9. **Tap Back to return to the server Settings screen.**
10. **In the Outgoing Mail Server section, type your account username in the User Name box and the account password in the Password box.**
11. **Tap Done.**

Configuring Email Messages

The rest of this chapter takes you through a few useful and timesaving techniques for handling email messages on your iPhone.

Creating iCloud message folders

In your email program on your computer, you've no doubt created a lot of folders to hold different types of messages that you want or need to save: projects, people, mailing list gems, and so on. This is a great way to reduce Inbox clutter and organize the email portion of your life.

Of course, these days the email portion of your life extends beyond your computer and probably includes a lot of time spent on your iPhone. Wouldn't it be great to have that same folder convenience and organization on your favorite phone? Happily, you can. If you have an iCloud account, any folders (technically, Apple calls them mailboxes) that you create on your iCloud account — either on your computer or on the iCloud site — are automatically mirrored on the iPhone Mail app.

Even better, you can create new iCloud message folders right from the comfort of your iPhone. Here's how:

1. **On the Home screen, tap Mail to open the Mail app.**
2. **Display the Mailboxes screen.**

3. **Tap Edit.** Mail opens the iCloud folders list for editing.
4. **Tap New Mailbox.**
5. **Type a name for the new folder.**
6. **Tap the Mailbox Location and then tap the iCloud folder in which you want to store your new folder.** If you want to create a new top-level folder, tap iCloud.
7. **Tap Save.** Mail adds the folder, and iCloud propagates the change to the cloud.
8. **Tap Done.**

Note

To move a message to your new folder, display the iCloud Inbox folder, tap the message, tap the Move icon (the folder), and then tap the new folder.

Attaching a file from iCloud Drive

If you've been using iCloud Drive to store documents in the cloud, you might need to share one of those documents with someone else over email. You'd normally log on to iCloud Drive to do this, but you can actually send an iCloud Drive file attachment directly from the comfort of your iPhone. Here's how it works.

1. **In Mail, start a new message, address it, and add a subject.**
2. **Tap and hold an empty section of the message for a few seconds.**
3. **In the menu that appears, tap More (the right-pointing arrow).**
4. **If you don't see the Add Document command, tap More a second time.**
5. **Tap Add Document.** Mail opens the iCloud Drive screen.
6. **Open a folder, if needed, and then tap the file.** Mail attaches the file to your message.

Formatting email text

We're all used to rich text email messages by now, where formatting such as bold and italics is used to add pizzazz or emphasis to our e-musings. iOS Mail gives you a limited set of formatting options for text: bold, italics, and underline. It's not much, but it's a start, so here are the steps to follow to format text in the Mail app:

1. **In your email message, tap within the word or phrase you want to format.** The Mail app displays the cursor.
2. **Tap the cursor.** Mail displays a set of options.

3. **Tap Select.** Mail selects the word closest to the cursor.
4. **If needed, drag the selection handles to select the entire phrase you want to format.** Mail displays a set of options for the selected text.
5. **Tap the arrow on the right side of the options.** Mail displays more options.
6. **Tap the BIU button.** Mail displays the Bold, Italics, and Underline buttons, as shown in Figure 6.4.

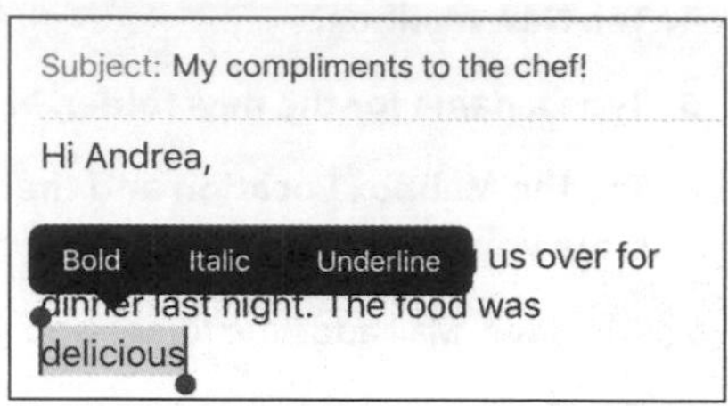

6.4 You can format email text with bold, italics, or underline.

7. **Tap the formatting you want to apply.** Mail leaves the formatting options on the screen, so feel free to apply multiple formats, if needed.
8. **Tap another part of the screen to hide the formatting options.**

Genius

If you're composing a message on your computer and decide to work on it later, your mail program stores the message as a draft that you can reopen any time. The Mail app doesn't *appear* to have that option, but it does. In the message window, tap Cancel (unintuitive, I know!) and then tap Save Draft. When you're ready to resume editing, open the account in the Mailboxes screen, tap Drafts, and then tap your saved message.

Creating a custom iPhone signature

Email signatures can range from the simple — a signoff such as "Cheers" or "All the best," followed by the sender's name — to baroque masterpieces filled with contact information, snappy quotations, and even text-based artwork! On your iPhone, the Mail app takes the simple route by adding the following signature to all your outgoing messages (new messages, replies, and forwards):

```
Sent from my iPhone
```

I like this signature because it's short, simple, and kind of cool (I, of course, *want* my recipients to know that I'm using my iPhone). If that default signature doesn't rock your world, you can create a custom one that does. Follow these steps:

1. **On the Home screen, tap Settings.** Your iPhone opens the Settings app.
2. **Tap Mail.** You see the Mail settings screen.
3. **Tap Signature.** The Signature screen appears.

4. **If you have multiple accounts and you prefer to create a unique signature for each one, tap Per Account.** If, instead, you leave the All Accounts item selected, Mail will use the same signature for all your accounts.
5. **Tap the default signature to open it for editing.** If you tapped Per Account in Step 4, tap the signature for the account you want to work with.
6. **Type the signature you want to use.** Mail saves your new signature as you type.

Disabling remote images in messages

A lot of messages nowadays come not just as plain text but with fonts, colors, images, and other flourishes. This fancy formatting, called either rich text or HTML, makes for a more pleasant email experience, particularly when using images in messages, because who doesn't like a bit of eye candy to brighten his day?

Unfortunately, getting images into your email messages can sometimes be problematic:

- **A cellular connection might cause trouble.** For example, it might take a long time to load the images, or if your data plan has an upper limit, you might not want a bunch of email images taking a big bite out of that limit.
- **Not all email images are benign.** A *web bug* is an image that resides on a remote server and is added to an HTML-formatted email message by referencing an address on the remote server. When you open the message, Mail uses the address to download the image for display within the message. That sounds harmless enough, but if the message is junk email, it's likely that the address also contains either your email address or a code that points to your email address. So, when the remote server gets a request to load the image, it knows not only that you've opened the message but also that your email address is legitimate. So, not surprisingly, spammers use web bugs all the time because, for them, valid email addresses are a form of gold.

Note

HTML, which stands for Hypertext Markup Language, is a set of codes that folks use to put together web pages.

The iPhone Mail app displays remote images by default. To disable remote images, follow these steps:

1. **On the Home screen, tap Settings.** Your iPhone opens the Settings app.
2. **Tap Mail.** You see the Mail settings screen.
3. **Tap the Load Remote Images switch to Off.** Mail saves the setting and no longer displays remote images in your email messages.

Preventing Mail from organizing messages by thread

In the Mail app, your messages get grouped by thread, which means the original message and all the replies you've received are grouped together in the account's Inbox folder. This is usually remarkably handy, because it means you don't have to scroll through a million messages to locate the reply you want to read.

Mail indicates a thread by displaying a circled arrow instead of just an arrow (>) to the right of the first message in the thread, as shown in Figure 6.5. Tap the message to see a list of the messages in the thread and then tap the message you want to read.

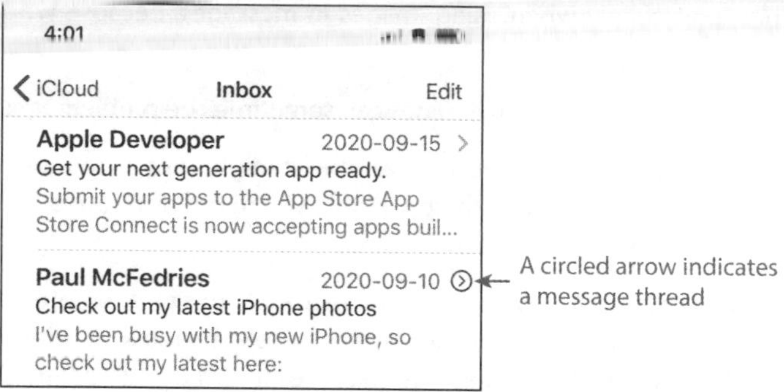

6.5 If you see a circled arrow on the right side of a message, that tells you there are multiple messages in the thread.

Organizing messages by thread is usually convenient, but not always. For example, sometimes you view your messages and scroll through them by tapping the Next (downward-pointing arrow) and Previous (upward-pointing arrow) buttons. When you come to a thread, Mail jumps into the thread, and you then scroll through each message in the thread, which can be a real hassle if the thread contains a large number of replies.

If you find that threads are more hassle than they're worth, you can follow these steps to configure Mail to no longer organize messages by thread:

1. **On the Home screen, tap Settings.** Your iPhone opens the Settings app.
2. **Tap Mail.** You see the Mail settings screen.
3. **Tap the Organize By Thread switch to Off.** Your iPhone saves the setting and no longer organizes your messages by thread.

Maintaining messages with gestures

If you have a long list of messages to process, Mail can help speed things up by enabling you to use gestures to perform basic message maintenance right from the account Inbox. Here's a summary:

- **To mark a message as read, swipe right on the message and then tap Read (see Figure 6.6).**

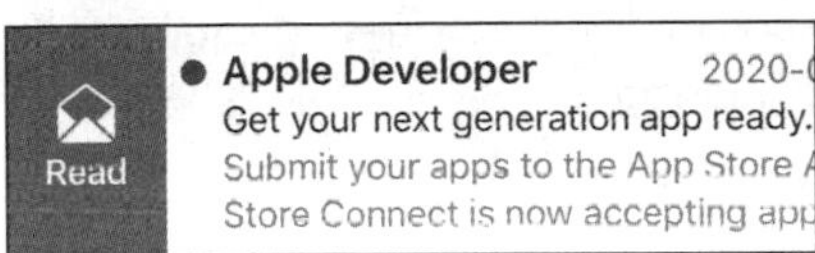

6.6 Swipe right on a message to mark it as read.

- **To flag a message, perform a short swipe left on the message and then tap Flag (see Figure 6.7).**

6.7 Swipe left on a message to flag it.

- **To see more message options, perform a short swipe left on the message and then tap More.** The menu that appears includes the commands Reply, Reply All, Forward, Trash, Flag, Mark as Read, Move Message, Archive Message, Move to Junk, Mute, and Notify Me.
- **To delete a message, either perform a short swipe left on the message and then tap Trash or perform a long swipe left on the message until it disappears from the Inbox.**

Configuring Mail's swipe options

You saw in the previous section that Mail can make processing your messages a lot easier by letting you use swipe gestures to mark messages as read and flag messages. Even better, you have a bit of control over which tasks Mail presents when you swipe:

1. **On the Home screen, tap Settings.** Your iPhone opens the Settings app.
2. **Tap Mail.** You see the Mail settings screen.
3. **Tap Swipe Options to open the Swipe Options screen.**

4. **Tap Swipe Left, tap the action you want to see when you swipe left, and then tap Swipe Options to return to the previous screen.**
5. **Tap Swipe Right, tap the action you want to see when you swipe right, and then tap Swipe Options to return to the previous screen.**

Marking all messages as read

You saw in the previous section that you can use a swipe-right gesture to mark a message as read right from the Inbox. This is no big whoop for five or ten messages, but a very big whoop indeed for dozens or even hundreds of messages.

Happily, that annoyance needn't be added to your iOS gripe list because the Mail app also gives you a simple way to mark *everything* as read in one (more or less) fell swoop:

1. **In the Mail app, open the mailbox you want to manage.**
2. **Tap Edit.** Mail puts the mailbox into Edit mode.
3. **Tap Select All.** Mail selects all the mailbox messages.
4. **Tap Mark.** Mail asks what you want marked.
5. **Tap Mark as Read.** Mail marks every message in the mailbox as having been read. Sweet!

Controlling email with Siri voice commands

You can use the Siri voice recognition app to check, compose, send, and reply to messages, all with simple voice commands. Tap and hold the Home button (or press and hold the Mic button of the iPhone headphones, or the equivalent button on a Bluetooth headset) until Siri appears.

To check for new email messages on your iCloud account, you need only say "Check email" (or just "Check mail"). You can also view a list of iCloud messages as follows:

- **Displaying unread messages.** Say "Show new email."
- **Displaying messages where the subject line contains a specified topic.** Say "Show email about *topic*," where *topic* is the topic you want to view.
- **Displaying messages from a particular person.** Say "Show email from *name*," where *name* is the name of the sender.

To start a new email message, Siri gives you a lot of options:

- **Creating a new message addressed to a particular person.** Say "Email *name*," where *name* is the name of the recipient. This name can be a name from your Contacts list or someone with a defined relationship, such as "Mom" or "my brother."

- **Creating a new message with a particular subject line.** Say "Email *name* about *subject*," where *name* defines the recipient, and *subject* is the subject line text.
- **Creating a new message with a particular body.** Say "Email *name* and say *text*," where *name* is the recipient and *text* is the message body text.

In each case, Siri creates the new message, displays it, and then asks if you want to send it. If you do, you can either say "Send" or tap the Send button.

If you have a message displayed, you can send a response by saying "Reply." If you want to add some text to the response, say "Reply *text*," where *text* is your response.

You can also use Siri within Mail to dictate a message. When you tap inside the body of a new message, the keyboard that appears shows a Mic icon beside the spacebar. Tap the Mic icon and then start dictating. Here are some notes:

- For punctuation, you can say the name of the mark you need, such as "comma" (,), "semicolon" (;), "colon" (:), "period" or "full stop" (.), "question mark" (?), "exclamation point" (!), "dash" (–), or "at sign" (@).
- You can enclose text in parentheses by saying "open parenthesis," then the text, and then "close parenthesis."
- To surround text with quotation marks, say "open quote," then the text, then "close quote."
- To render a word in all uppercase letters, say "all caps" and then say the word.
- To start a new paragraph, say "new line."
- You can have some fun by saying "smiley face" for :-), "winky face" for ;-), and "frowny face" for :-(.
- To spell out a word (such as "period" or "colon"), say "No caps on, no space on," spell the word, and then say "No space off, no caps off."

When you're finished, tap Done.

How Do I Max Out My iPhone's Photo and Video Features?

One of the more interesting ways the iPhone has evolved since its release in 2007 is that it has gone from initially being a phone that happens to have a camera, to being a camera that happens to have a phone. Before that evolution took place, only a few die-hard shutterbugs and trip-documenting tourists lugged around a camera. Now *everyone* takes photos constantly. Go to any reasonably interesting scene or event, and at least half the viewers will have iPhones in front of their faces snapping pics. The basics of using the iPhone's cameras are fairly straightforward to learn, but these cameras are now extremely sophisticated devices, so there's much more to learn beyond those basics. This chapter takes you there by showing you not only how to take pictures and videos, but how to enhance and work with photos and videos, right on your phone.

Taking Great iPhone Pictures

Your iPhone comes with a couple of built-in digital cameras that you can use to take pictures while you're running around town. Taking a picture is straightforward. First, on the Home screen, tap Camera. (Alternatively, from any screen, display the Control Center and then tap the Camera icon.) If this is the first time you've opened the Camera app, it asks if it can use your current location. This is an excellent idea because it tags your photos with your present whereabouts, so be sure to tap OK.

Genius

When your iPhone is locked, you can get to the Camera app lickety-split by waking up your phone and then swiping left (or by pressing the Camera icon for a couple of seconds).

Taking a basic photo

When the Camera app appears, follow these steps to take a basic photo:

1. **Make sure the Mode switch (pointed out later in Figure 7.1) is on Photo.**
2. **If you're taking a selfie, tap the Switch Camera button to use the front camera.**
3. **Line up your shot on the screen.**
4. **Take the photo using either of the following techniques:**
   - Tap the Shutter button (which, again, I point out in Figure 7.1).
   - Tap the Volume Up switch, which appears on the top edge of the iPhone when you hold it in the landscape position with the notch on the right (or the Home button on the left).
5. **To view your photo, tap the Camera Roll button, which appears in the lower-left corner of the Camera app screen (see Figure 7.1).**

Genius

When you first launch the Camera app, it asks whether it can use your current location. In the case of the Camera app, if you allow this, it means the app accesses your location only while you're using the app. You can control this — that is, you can toggle geotagging on and off — by launching the Settings app, tapping Privacy, tapping Location Services, tapping Camera, and then tapping an option: Never, Ask Next Time, or While Using the App.

7.1 The most important camera features.

Checking out the iPhone camera features

You'll no doubt want to go beyond the basic photo-taking steps of the previous section to make the most of the sophisticated camera you hold in your hands. The best way to do that is to get to know the most useful and most powerful camera features. I point these out in Figure 7.1 and then talk more about each one in the sections that follow.

7.2 Tap More (see Figure 7.1) to see some extra camera controls.

Tapping the More button (the upward-pointing arrow pointed out in Figure 7.1) replaces the Mode switch with the extra camera controls shown in Figure 7.2.

Focusing the shot

The iPhone cameras automatically focus on whatever subject is in the middle of the frame. This Autofocus feature is usually what you want, but if the subject you'd prefer to focus on is not in the middle of the frame, you can tap the subject and the Camera app automatically moves the focus to that object. It also automatically adjusts the white balance and exposure. The Camera app marks the new focus location by displaying a square like the one shown in Figure 7.3.

7.3 Tap the screen to set that location as the focus of the photo.

Caution

Once you've tapped to set the focus, don't move the phone too much or the Camera app will refocus on any new subject that comes into the center of the frame.

Locking the focus and exposure

Tap-to-focus is a handy feature, except when you've got the perfect shot lined up and Autofocus kicks in and wrecks the focus or exposure (or both!). To prevent this, compose your shot and then tap and hold on the person or object you want to focus on for about 3 seconds (or until the focus rectangle pulses). When you release your finger, you see AE/AF Lock (short for AutoExposure/AutoFocus) at the top of the screen, as shown in Figure 7.4. Your current focus and exposure settings are now locked. Fire away!

7.4 Tap and hold for a few seconds to lock the focus and exposure.

Shooting in low light with Night Mode

If you have an iPhone 11 or newer, you get a camera feature called Night Mode, which takes a series of images at different exposures to create low-light or night scenes that have amazing detail and clarity. Night Mode works automatically, meaning that your camera detects the amount of light available, turns on Night Mode if the amount of light is low, and then sets the number of seconds for the exposure. You see the Night Mode indicator in the top-left corner of the Camera app, along with the time of the exposure (usually just a second or two, but it can be up to 30 seconds!), as shown in Figure 7.5. If you prefer to adjust the exposure time manually, tap the Night Mode button and then set the exposure time using the Night Mode control.

Night mode is on with a 1-second exposure

Night Mode control

7.5 Tap the Night Mode button to set the exposure time manually.

Caution

Your iPhone uses optical image stabilization to allow for a bit of camera shake while the Night Mode photo is taken, but you should still try to keep the phone as steady as you can while the Camera app takes the shot, particularly for multiple-second exposures.

Note

The iPhone has a built-in LED flash that sits right beside the rear camera, so you can take pictures at night or in extremely low-light conditions with any iPhone. For an iPhone 11 or newer, however, the Camera app switches automatically between using the flash or using Night Mode. If the iPhone enables the flash but you'd prefer to use Night Mode, tap the Flash button (pointed out in Figure 7.1) to turn off the flash and switch to Night Mode.

Taking live photos

Live Photos (which is automatically enabled on most iPhones) takes a series of still images for 1.5 seconds before and after you press the Shutter button. The result is a special animated JPEG image that, when pressed and held, displays these images sequentially, resulting in what appears to be a 3-second video clip. To turn off this feature, tap the Live Photos button (pointed out earlier in Figure 7.1).

Taking a portrait photo

When you want to take a portrait of a person or pet, the Camera app's Portrait mode is the way to go because it automatically configures two camera settings for idea portraits:

- It switches the zoom level to 2x, which is ideal for head shots.
- It decreases the depth of field to blur the background, which brings more attention to your subject.

Here are the steps to follow to take a portrait photo:

1. **Use the Mode switch (pointed out earlier in Figure 7.1) to select Portrait.**
2. **Use the Portrait Lighting control (see Figure 7.6) to select the lighting effect you want to use.**
3. **To change the depth of field, tap the Depth of Field icon (see Figure 7.6) and then set the f-stop value you want:**
   - For a clearer background, choose a higher f-stop value.
   - For a blurrier background, choose a lower f-stop value.

Genius

An *f-stop* is a number that specifies the size of a camera's aperture (the opening that determines how much light gets to the lens). The higher the f-stop value, the smaller the aperture (and vice versa). The iPhone camera aperture isn't physically changeable. Instead, the effect of changing the f-stop is simulated in software.

Depth of Field

NATURAL LIGHT

Portrait Lighting

7.6 Tap and hold for a few seconds to lock the focus and exposure.

4. **Line up your subject on the screen.**
5. **Make sure the camera isn't too close (at least a couple of feet away) or too far (no more than 7 or 8 feet away).** If you're too close, the Camera app tells you to move farther away; if you're too far away, the Camera app tells you to move closer.
6. **Take the photo.**

Note

If you're not sure about which lighting effect you want to use or which depth of field setting is right, don't worry about it too much because you can always adjust both settings later in the Photos app. Open the photo and then tap the Portrait icon (which I point out later in Figure 7.10).

Taking a panoramic photo

One of the biggest challenges all photographers face is capturing very wide shots, particularly landscapes. If you have a high-end digital SLR camera, you can swap out your regular lens for a wide-angle lens, but that's not an option with the iPhone. However, the Camera app does offer the next best thing: the Panorama feature. Panorama uses the iPhone's built-in three-axis gyroscope to precisely align the images as you shoot them, even if the iPhone shakes or your pan isn't perfectly straight. The result is a seamless panoramic view of up to 240 degrees (up to a maximum image resolution of 63 megapixels on recent iPhone models).

Follow these steps to take a panoramic photo:

1. **On the Home screen, tap Camera.** The Camera app appears.
2. **Use the Mode switch to select Pano.** Camera displays the Panorama tool, shown in Figure 7.7.
3. **Position the iPhone so that the camera is pointing at the leftmost part of the panoramic scene you want to capture.** If you'd prefer to pan from right to left instead, tap the arrow to reverse the direction.
4. **Tap the Shutter button to begin the shot.**
5. **Pan the iPhone, keeping the following pointers in mind:**
   - Pan the iPhone steadily and continuously.
   - Don't pan too fast. If you see "Slow down" on the screen, it means you're panning too quickly.
   - Don't pan in the opposite direction or Camera will end the shot.
   - Try to keep the arrow centered on the horizontal line.
   - If the arrow falls below the line, either raise the iPhone or tilt the top of the iPhone toward you.
   - If the arrow moves above the line, either lower the iPhone or tilt the top of the iPhone away from you.
6. **When your panorama is complete, tap Done.** Camera also stops the shot automatically if you pan a full 240 degrees. Camera stitches together the shots and saves the panorama to the Camera Roll.

7.7 Use the Mode switch to select Pano to see the Panorama tool.

Changing the zoom level

The *zoom level* is a measure of how much the camera magnifies the current scene:

- A zoom level of 1x displays the screen normally.
- A zoom level greater than 1x magnifies the scene to get a narrower view.
- A zoom level between 0.5x and 1x pulls out from the scene to get a wider view.

The Camera app sets the zoom level automatically to 1x, except when you switch to Portrait mode, in which case the Camera app sets the zoom level to 2x. However, you can set the zoom level manually by tapping and holding the Zoom level controls (see Figure 7.1), then using the dial that appears to set the zoom level you want, as shown in Figure 7.8.

7.8 Tap and hold the zoom level controls and then use this dial to set your custom zoom level.

Changing the aspect ratio

The *aspect ratio* is the ratio of a photo's height to its width (when the photo is taken with the phone in portrait orientation). The default aspect ratio is 4:3, but you can also choose either 16:9 or Square (that is, 1:1).

When you're about to take a photo, follow these steps to change the aspect ratio:

1. **Tap the More button, pointed out earlier in Figure 7.1.**
2. **Tap the Aspect Ratio button, pointed out earlier in Figure 7.2.**
3. **Tap the aspect ratio you want: Square, 4:3, or 16:9.**

Applying a filter

The stunning popularity of the Instagram app and similar apps such as Hipstamatic has created a mania for applying filters to photos. A *filter* is a special effect applied to a photo's colors to give it a different feel. The Camera app comes with a Filters icon (see Figure 7.2), as does the Photos app in Edit mode. When you tap Filters, you see nine effects that you can apply to your photo, including Mono (which gives you a black-and-white photo).

Follow these steps to apply a filter before you take a photo:

1. **Tap the More button, pointed out earlier in Figure 7.1.**
2. **Tap the Filters button, pointed out earlier in Figure 7.2.**
3. **Tap the filter you want to apply.**

Taking a time-delayed photo

The term *selfie* (that is, a photo that you take of yourself, possibly with a friend or two included) is now a permanent part of the lexicon, which I'm sure isn't even remotely shocking news to you. You only have to look around at any event or occasion to realize that each of us has become our favorite photo subject. To make selfies even easier to shoot, just switch to the iPhone's front camera, which seems nearly tailor-made for taking selfies.

I say "nearly" because the front camera method for taking selfies does come with a significant drawback: All shots must be taken more or less at arm's length, which gives every such photo a characteristic "This is me taking a selfie" look.

Creative selfie-takers have worked around these limitations by using mirrors, selfie-sticks, and other tricks, but the Camera app offers a simpler alternative: time-delay. This feature tells Camera to wait for several seconds after you tap the Shutter button before taking the photo. This means your photo-taking steps change as follows:

1. **Use Switch Camera to select the camera you want to use.**
2. **Tap the Time Delay button (see Figure 7.2) and then tap the number of seconds you want to use for the delay: 3 seconds or 10 seconds.**
3. **Position the iPhone (on, say, a desk or chair) so that it's pointing toward the scene you want to shoot.**
4. **Tap Shutter.**
5. **Scurry into the frame before the shot is taken.**

Note that the Camera app takes not one photo, but a burst of 11 photos. To choose what photo you want to keep, tap Camera Roll, tap Select, tap the photo you want to keep, tap Done, and then tap Keep Only 1 Favorite.

Genius

Burst mode isn't only available when you're taking time-delayed photos. You can snap a burst of photos any time you want by tapping and holding the Shutter button. If you have an iPhone 11 or newer, you use a different technique: Swipe left on the Shutter button and then hold your finger on the screen until you want the burst to end; then lift your finger.

Taking time-lapse photos

If you want to document a scene that's changing, the two standard-issue techniques are to take a new photo every so often and to switch to video mode and shoot the entire scene. These techniques work well enough, but it's a pain to have to remember to take individual shots, and for a scene that's changing slowly, a video might be overkill.

In many such cases a better solution is to use Time Lapse mode, which creates a video of a scene by automatically taking a picture every second or so. This saves you the hassle of taking individual shots as well as the storage space required for a full-blown video.

To take time-lapse photos, set the Mode switch to Time Lapse and then tap the Shutter button.

Preventing blurry iPhone photos

The iPhone camera hardware is gradually getting better, and the iPhone generally takes really nice shots. However, probably the biggest problem most people have with iPhone photos is blurry images, which are caused by not holding the phone steady while taking the shot.

The latest iPhones offer optical image stabilization, but still there are a few other things you can do to minimize or ideally eliminate blurred shots:

- Widen your stance to stabilize your body.
- Lean your shoulder (at least) or your entire side (at best) against any nearby object, such as a wall, doorframe, or car.
- Place your free arm across your torso with your forearm parallel to the ground; then rest the elbow of your "shooting" arm (that is, the one holding the iPhone) on the free arm, which should help steady your shooting arm.
- Hold your breath while taking the shot.
- Remember that your iPhone takes the shot when you *release* the Shutter button, not when you *press* it. Therefore, keep your subject composed and yourself steadied as best you can until you lift your finger off the Shutter button.

Caution

You might be tempted to press and hold the Shutter button and release it only when you're steady. Unfortunately, that technique no longer works because pressing and holding the Shutter button initiates either quick video recording (in iPhone 11 or newer) or burst mode.

- After you release the Shutter button, keep the phone steady until the photo thumbnail appears in the lower-left corner of the screen. If you move while the iPhone is finalizing the photo, you'll blur the shot.

Keep some or all of these pointers in mind while shooting with your iPhone, and you'll soon find that blurry iPhone photos are a thing of the past.

Getting More Out of iPhone Photos

You can do quite a lot with your photos after they're in your iPhone, but first you have to get to them: Tap the Photos icon on your iPhone Home screen. The Photos app displays the Photos tab, as shown in Figure 7.9, which lists all your photos, with the most recent at the bottom. You can tap Years, Months, or Days to organize your photos by those time frames. Tap a time frame to see its pictures and then tap the picture you want to check out.

7.9 The Photos app is the place to view and work with your iPhone photos.

You can also use the tabs at the bottom of the app to navigate your photos:

- **Photos.** This is the default tab that displays all your photos.
- **For You.** This displays a few curated images that the Photos app thinks might interest you.

- **Albums.** This organizes your photos into albums. I talk about creating photo albums a bit later in this chapter.
- **Search.** This enables you to search for a photo using keywords such as *dog* or *car*, the name of a person, or the name of a location.

Scrolling, rotating, zooming, and panning photos

You can use the following techniques to navigate and manipulate your photos:

- **Scroll.** You move forward or backward through your photos by flicking. Flick up or down to navigate the thumbnails. When you've finished viewing an individual image, flick from the right to left to view the next photo; flick left to right to view the previous shot.
- **Rotate.** When a landscape shot shows up on your iPhone, it gets letterboxed at the top (that is, you see white space above and below the image). To get a better view, rotate the screen into the landscape position and the photo rotates right along with it, filling most of the screen. When you come upon a photo with a portrait orientation, rotate the iPhone back to the upright position for best viewing.
- **Zoom.** Zooming magnifies the shot that's on the screen. There are two methods you can use:
  - **Double-tap the area of the photo on which you want to zoom in.** The iPhone doubles the size of the portion you tapped. Double-tap again to return the photo to its original size.
  - **Spread and pinch.** To zoom in, place two fingers on the screen over the area you want magnified and spread them apart. To zoom back out, pinch two fingers together.
- **Pan.** After you zoom in on the photo, you may find that the iPhone didn't zoom in exactly where you wanted or you may just want to see another part of the photo. Drag your finger across the screen to move the photo along with your finger — an action known as *panning*.

Note

You can scroll to another photo if you're zoomed in, but it takes a lot more work to get there because the iPhone thinks you're trying to pan. For faster scrolling, return the photo to its normal size by double-tapping the screen and then scroll.

Enhancing a photo

Don't worry if you have a photo that's too bright in some spots or if the color is washed out in others — the Photos app comes with an Enhance tool that can automatically adjust the color and brightness. Here's how to use it:

1. **In the Photos app, open the photo you want to fix.**
2. **Tap the photo to display the controls.**
3. **Tap Edit.** The Photos app displays its editing tools.
4. **Tap Enhance (the magic wand icon).** The Photos app adjusts the color and brightness.
5. **Tap Done.** The Photos app saves your changes.

Cropping and straightening

If you have a photo containing elements that you don't want or need to see, you can often cut them out. This is called *cropping*, and you can use the Photos app to do it. When you crop a photo, you specify a rectangular area of the image that you want to keep. The Photos app then discards everything outside of the rectangle. Cropping is a useful skill because it can help you give focus to the true subject of a photo. Cropping is also useful for removing extraneous elements that appear on or near the edges of a photo.

As you probably know from hard-won experience, getting an iPhone camera perfectly level when you take a shot is difficult. It requires a lot of practice and a steady hand. Despite your best efforts, you might still end up with a photo that is not quite level. To fix this problem, you can also use the Photos app to rotate the photo clockwise or counterclockwise so that the subject appears straight.

Genius

If your iPhone photos are consistently askew, turn on the Camera grid, which adds lines that divide the Camera screen into nine rectangles (that is, a 3 x 3 grid). Open the Settings app, tap Photos & Camera, and then tap the Grid switch to On. The grid is also useful for composing pictures using the Rule of Thirds, where you place your subject on one of the grid lines instead of in the middle of the screen.

Follow these steps to crop and straighten a photo:

1. **In the Photos app, open the photo that you want to edit.**
2. **Tap the photo to display the controls.**
3. **Tap Edit.** The Photos app displays its editing tools.

4. **Tap Crop (see Figure 7.10).** The Photos app displays a grid for cropping and straightening, as shown in Figure 7.10.

5. **Tap and drag a corner of the grid to set the area you want to keep.**

6. **To straighten the photo, tap Straighten and then drag the ruler (see Figure 7.10) left or right until the image is level.** Note, too, that Photos also offers Tilt Vertical and Tilt Horizontal tools (see Figure 7.10) that you can use to tilt your photo as needed.

7. **Tap Done.** The Photos app applies the changes to the photo.

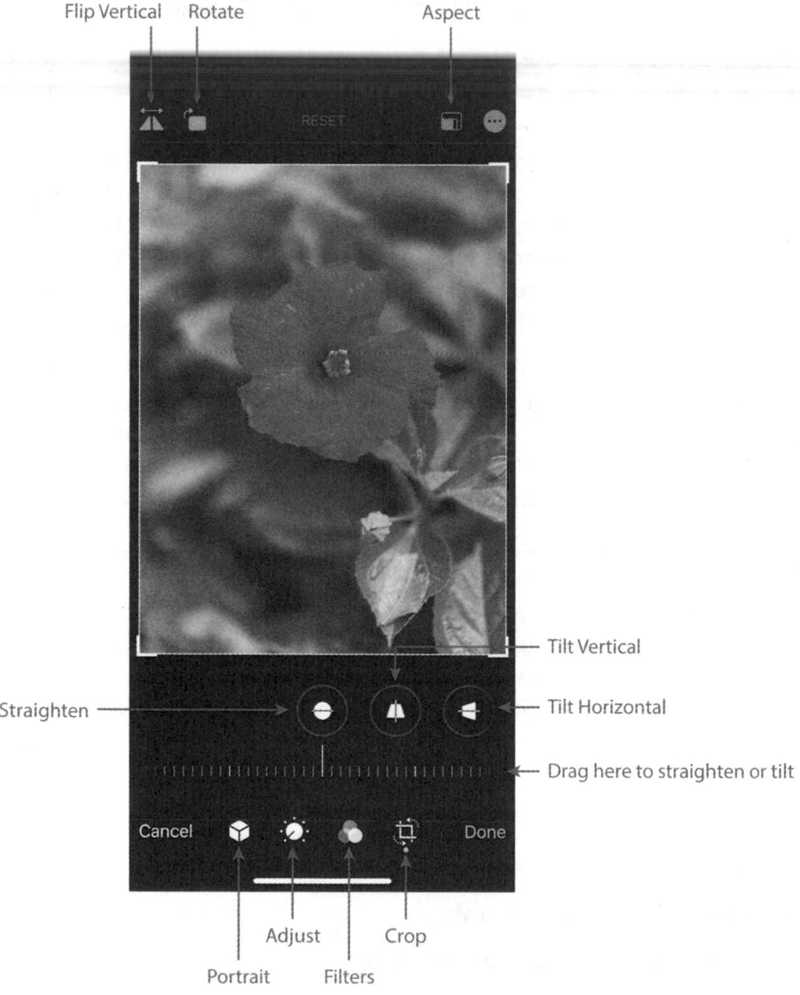

7.10 Tap Crop to display the cropping and straightening tools.

Genius

The fastest way to crop some photos is to tell the Photos app the dimensions you want to use for the resulting photo. Tap Aspect (pointed out in Figure 7.10) and then tap either a specific shape (Original or Square) or a specific ratio, such as 5:7 or 8:10. You then drag the photo (not the grid!) so the portion you want to keep is within the grid.

Note

The Crop feature also enables you to rotate a photo 90 degrees, say, from portrait to landscape. To do this, tap the Rotate icon (see Figure 7.10) until the photo is in the orientation you want. You can also tap Flip Vertical (see Figure 7.10) to flip the photo along the vertical axis.

Applying a filter

Earlier I talked about how to apply a filter while you take a photo. However, you can also apply a filter after the fact by following these steps in the Photos app:

1. **Open the photo you want to edit.**
2. **Tap the photo to display the controls.**
3. **Tap Edit.** The Photos app displays its editing tools.
4. **Tap Filters (pointed out in Figure 7.10).** Photos displays thumbnail versions of the photo that demonstrate each effect.
5. **Tap the effect you want to use.**
6. **Tap Done.** The Photos app applies the filter to the photo.

Adjusting a photo's lighting

Even if you take quite a bit of care setting up and taking your shot, you might still end up with a photo that is under- or over-exposed, has shadows that are too dark or too light, or has poor overall contrast. If the lighting in a photo is off, the Photos app offers a huge number of settings that you can use to make adjustments. However, for most photos you can get things to look the way you want by adjusting one or more of the following:

- **Contrast.** Use this slider to adjust the distribution of the photo's tones. If the tones in your photo are starkly different, lower the contrast to make them more alike; if your photo is bland because the tones are all alike, increase the contrast to make the tones stand out.

- **Exposure.** Use this slider to set the overall lighting of the photo. If your entire photo is washed out because it's too light, decrease the exposure to get a darker image; if your entire photo is muddy because it's too dark, increase the exposure to get a lighter image.
- **Highlights.** Use this slider to adjust how intense the brightest parts of the image appear. If your photo has one or more areas that are washed out because they're too bright, reduce the Highlights value to counter that effect.
- **Shadows.** Use this slider to adjust how intense the darkest parts of the image appear. If your photo has one or more areas that show no detail because they're too dark, reduce the Shadows value to try and bring back some of that detail.

Here are the steps to follow:

1. **Open the photo you want to adjust.**
2. **Tap the photo to display the controls.**
3. **Tap Edit.** The Photos app displays its editing tools.
4. **Tap Adjust (pointed out in Figure 7.10).** Photos displays the lighting adjustment controls.
5. **Tap the control you want to use and then drag the ruler to adjust the lighting.**
6. **Repeat Step 5 for each lighting adjustment you want to apply.**
7. **Tap Done.** The Photos app applies the lighting adjustments to the photo.

Note

To remove a custom album you no longer need, tap Albums, tap Edit, tap the red Delete icon to the left of the custom album, tap the Delete button that appears, and then tap Delete Album when Photos asks you to confirm.

Creating a photo album

Normally you'd use your computer to organize your photos into albums prior to syncing them to your iPhone. However, if you have been taking a lot of pictures on your iPhone and your computer is nowhere in sight, you don't have to wait to organize your pics. The Photos app enables you to create your own photo albums right on your iPhone. These albums aren't transferred to your computer when you sync, but they're handy if you need to organize your photos quickly. Here's what you do:

1. **In the Photos app, tap Albums.** The Albums screen appears. If you see an album instead, tap Albums in the upper-left corner.
2. **Tap the Add (+) button.** The Photos app prompts you for an album name.
3. **Type the name and then tap Save.** Photos displays the Moments collection, which organizes your photos by date and location.
4. **Tap each image that you want to include in your new album.** A check mark appears next to each photo you select.
5. **Tap Done.** The Photos app creates the new album, adds it to the Albums screen, and populates it with the photos you selected.

Getting More Out of iPhone Videos

Most iPhone models have cameras that support 4K (3840 x 2160) recording at 24, 30, or 60 frames per second (fps), 1080p HD recording at 30 or 60 fps, and 720p HD recording at 30 fps. Most iPhones also come with a video stabilization feature that helps to reduce shaky shots and a Slo-Mo video setting that captures 1080p video at 120 or 240 fps.

Note

The *p* in horizontal resolution values such as 1080p and 720p stands for *progressive scanning*, which means each horizontal line in a frame is drawn in sequence (as opposed to *interlaced scanning*, which draws odd-numbered lines first and then even-numbered lines).

Recording video with an iPhone camera

Any smartphone worthy of the name should do all the things you need it to do during the course of your busy life, and one of the things you probably want to do is record events, happenings, moments, or just whatever is going on. Sure, a picture is worth the proverbial thousand words, but at 24, 30, or even 60 frames per second, a video is worth a lot more than that.

Caution

The high-definition (HD) video recording capabilities of the iPhone are so welcome that you might start shooting everything in sight. Be my guest! However, just be aware that your iPhone churns through disk space at the rapid rate of 17 Mbps when shooting 1080p video at 30 fps, which means each minute of video carves out nearly 130MB of disk real estate. 4K video is even more space-consuming, taking up about 350MB for every minute of 30 fps video.

Genius

You can cut the amount of space taken up by videos approximately in half by using Apple's High Efficiency format. iOS uses this format by default, but you should check to make sure: Open Settings, tap Camera, tap Formats, and then tap High Efficiency. Most newer devices and computers support this format, so you shouldn't have any trouble sharing your videos. If you do run into problems, you can always switch to the Most Compatible format.

And, this being an iPhone and all, it's no surprise that recording a video is almost criminally easy. Here's what you do:

1. **On the Home screen, tap Camera.** The Camera screen appears.
2. **Flick the Mode switch to Video (or Slo-Mo).**
3. **In the upper-right corner of the screen, tap the frame rate you want to use (24, 30, or 60).**
4. **Tap the zoom level you want to use.**
5. **Tap the Switch Camera icon if you want to use the front camera rather than the rear camera.**
6. **Tap the screen to focus the video, if necessary.**
7. **Tap the Record button.** Your iPhone starts recording video and displays the elapsed recording time at the top of the screen.
8. **If you want to take a still photo while you're recording the video, tap the Shutter icon in the lower-left corner of the screen.**
9. **When you're done, tap the Record button again to stop the recording.** Your iPhone saves the video to the Camera Roll.

Setting the recording format for video and slo-mo

As mentioned earlier, most iPhones can take all things video up a notch by recording at 60 fps. This produces super-smooth video motion, especially when filming fast-moving objects. The downside is that each minute of 4K 60 fps video eats up about 400MB of disk space.

If you're filming people or objects that are going really fast, you might want to slow things *way* down and record them in slow motion. In that case, your iPhone drops the resolution down to 1080p, but ups the frame rate to 120 fps. It's a beautiful effect, but it consumes disk space at a rate of 31 Mbps, or about 230MB per minute. Lots of free space to burn, you say? Well, in that case you can crank up (or is it down?) the slo-mo to 720p at 240 fps, which can capture even the fastest motion smoothly. The disk cost, in case you're wondering, is 42 Mbps, or about 315MB per minute. (There's are also a High Efficiency format that can shoot 1080p at 240 fps, which eats disk space at 480MB per minute.)

Here are the steps to follow to select a recording format for regular and slo-mo video:

1. **On the Home screen, tap Settings.** The Settings app loads.
2. **Tap Camera.**
3. **To set the video format, tap Record Video, tap the format — such as 1080p HD at 30 fps or 4K at 60 fps — and then tap Camera to return.**
4. **To set the slo-mo format, tap Record Slo-mo, tap the format — 1080p HD at 120 fps, 720p HD at 240 fps, or 1080p HD at 240 fps (High Efficiency) — and then tap Camera to return.**

Editing recorded video

Being able to record video at the tap of a button is pretty cool, but your iPhone tops that by also letting you perform basic editing chores right on the phone. (Insert sound of jaw hitting floor here.) It's nothing fancy — basically, you can trim video from the beginning and end of the file — but it sure beats having to first sync the video to your computer and then fire up iMovie or some other video-editing software.

Here's how to edit a video right on your iPhone:

1. **Open the Camera Roll album:**
   - **Camera app.** Tap the Camera Roll button in the lower-left corner of the screen.
   - **Photos app.** Display the Albums screen and then tap Videos in the Media Types section.
2. **Tap the video you want to edit.** The Photos app displays the video.
3. **Tap Edit.** Photos displays a timeline of the video along the bottom of the screen.
4. **Tap and drag the left edge of the timeline to set the starting point of the video.**

5. **Tap and drag the right edge of the timeline to set the ending point of the video.** The trimmed timeline appears surrounded by yellow. Figure 7.11 shows a video with the starting and ending trim points set.

7.11 Use the video timeline to set the start and end points of the video footage you want to keep.

Note

Video thumbnails show a video camera icon in the lower-left corner and the duration of the video in the lower-right corner.

6. **Tap Play to ensure you've set the start and end points correctly.** If not, repeat Steps 4 and 5 to adjust the timeline as needed.
7. **Tap Done.** Your iPhone asks whether you want to trim the original or save the trimmed version as a new clip.
8. **Tap either Save Video (to modify the original) or Save Video as New Clip (to create a new video from the trim).** Your iPhone trims the video and then saves your work.

Genius

If you need more precision when trimming the timeline, tap and hold either the start trim control or the end trim control. Your iPhone expands the timeline to show more frames, which enables you to make more precise edits.

Playing iPhone videos on your TV

You can carry a bunch of videos with you on your iPhone, so why shouldn't you be able to play them on a TV if you want? That's a good question; you can indeed connect your phone to your TV. You have to buy another cable, but that's the only investment you have to make to watch iPhone videos right on your TV.

You have two choices:

- **Apple Lightning Digital AV Adapter.** This $49 cable has a Lightning connector on one end to attach your iPhone, and an HDMI connector at the other end to attach an HDMI cable that in turn connects to your TV's HDMI input port.
- **Apple Lightning to VGA Adapter.** This $49 cable has a Lightning connector on one end, and a VGA connector on the other to attach a VGA cable that connects to your TV's VGA input port.

The cable you choose depends on the type of TV you have. Older sets have composite inputs, more recent TVs have component inputs, and the latest sets have at least one HDMI port.

After connecting your cables, set your TV to the input and play your videos as you normally would.

Streaming iPhone video to Apple TV

If you have an Apple TV that supports AirPlay, you can use AirPlay to stream a video from your iPhone to your TV. Here's how it works:

1. **Make sure your Apple TV is turned on.**
2. **On your iPhone, start the video you want to stream.**
3. **Swipe up from the bottom of the screen to display the Control Center.**
4. **Tap AirPlay.** Your iPhone displays a menu of output choices.
5. **Tap the name of your Apple TV device.** Your iPhone streams the video to that device, and hence to your TV.

Mirroring the iPhone screen on your TV

You can set up a *mirrored* display, which means that what you see on your iPhone is also displayed on your TV in HD. One way to do this is to use the Apple Lightning Digital AV Adapter or the Apple 30-pin Digital AV Adapter to connect your iPhone to your TV's HDMI port. However, iOS also offers wireless AirPlay mirroring through Apple TV. As long as you have a second-generation Apple TV (and it has been updated with the latest software), you can use AirPlay mirroring to send not only videos to your TV but also photos, slide shows, web sites, apps, games, and anything else you can display on your iPhone.

Follow these steps to start mirroring the iPhone screen on your TV:

1. **Turn on your Apple TV device.**
2. **On your iPhone, display the Control Center.**
3. **Tap the Screen Mirroring control.** Your iPhone displays the Screen Mirroring dialog, which offers a menu of output choices.
4. **Tap the name of your Apple TV device.**

Can I Use My iPhone to Manage Contacts and Appointments?

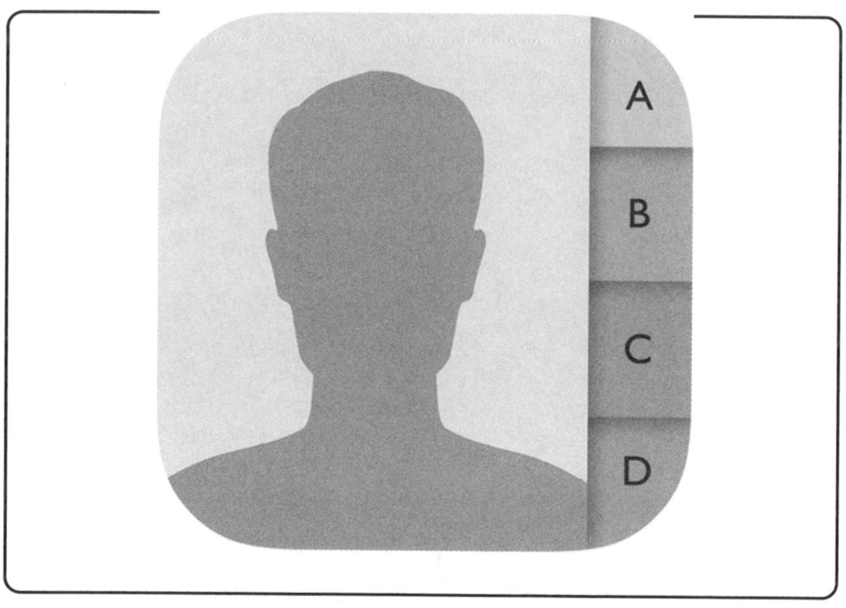

The iPhone has never just been about the technology. Yes, it looks stylish, it has enough bells and whistles to cause deafness, and it just works. iPhone users don't know or care about things like antennae, flash drives, memory chips, and whatever else Apple somehow managed to cram into that tiny case. These things don't matter because iPhone has always been about helping you get things done and making your life better, more creative, and more efficient. And, as you'll see in this chapter, your iPhone can also go a long way toward making your life — particularly your contacts and your calendar — more organized.

Managing Your Contacts

One of the paradoxes of modern life is that as contact information becomes more important, you store less and less of it in the easiest database system of all — your memory. Instead of memorizing phone numbers like you used to, you now store your contact info electronically. When you think about it, this isn't exactly surprising. It's not just a landline phone number that you have to remember for each person anymore but also a mobile number, email and web site addresses, a Twitter username, a physical address, and more. That's a lot to remember, so it makes sense to go the electronic route. And for the iPhone, *electronic* means the Contacts app, which seems basic enough but is actually loaded with useful features that can help you get organized and get the most out of the contact management side of your life.

Creating a new contact

Here are the steps to follow to create a new contact using the Contacts app:

1. **In the Home screen, tap the Contacts icon.** The Contacts app appears. If you're in the Phone app, you can also tap the Contacts button at the bottom of the screen.
2. **Tap the New Contact (+) button at the top-right corner of the screen.** The New Contact screen appears, as shown in Figure 8.1.
3. **Tap the First Name box and then type the person's first name.** If you're jotting down the contact data for a company or some other inanimate object, skip to Step 5.
4. **Tap the Last Name box and then type the person's surname.**
5. **If you want to note where the person works (or if you're adding a business to your Contacts app), tap the Company box and type the company name.**

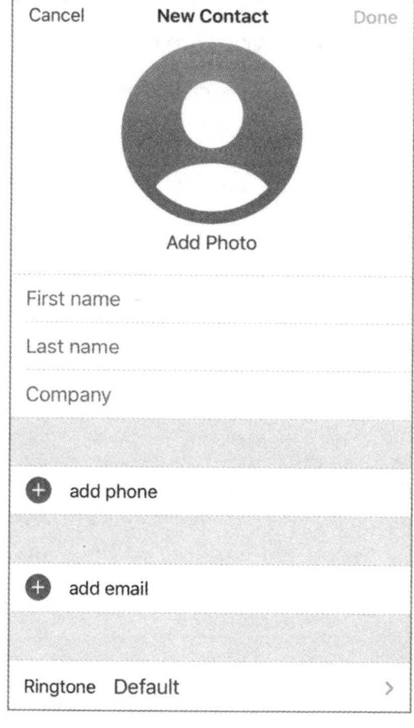

8.1 Use the New Contact screen to type the person's name and company name.

6. **To enter one or more phone numbers, follow these substeps:**
   a. Tap Add Phone.
   b. Tap the label (the default for the first phone number is Home) and then tap a label that best represents the type of phone number you're entering (such as Work or Mobile).
   c. Enter the contact's phone number.
   d. To add another phone number, repeat Steps a through c.
7. **To enter one or more email addresses, follow these substeps:**
   a. Tap Add Email.
   b. Tap the label (the default for the first email address is Home) and then tap a label that best represents the type of email address you're adding (such as Work or School).
   c. Enter the contact's email address.
   d. To add another email address, repeat Steps a through c.
8. **To add more data, tap Add *Type*, where *Type* is the type of data (such as URL, Address, or Birthday), choose a label, and then enter the data.** To access even more data types, tap Add Field to see a long list of extra types, such as Job Title, Middle Name, and Nickname. Tap a type to add it to the contact.
9. **Repeat Step 8 for all the data you want to add for the contact.**
10. **Tap Done.** Contacts saves the new contact and returns you to the Contacts screen.

Editing an existing contact

Here are the steps required to open an existing contact for editing:

1. **In Contacts, tap the contact you want to edit.**
2. **Tap Edit.** Contacts displays the contact's data.
3. **Make your changes.**
4. **Tap Done.** Contacts saves your work and returns you to the Contacts screen.

Adding a photo to a contact

You can assign a photo from one of your albums to any of your contacts by following these steps:

1. **In Contacts, tap the contact you want to edit.**
2. **Tap Edit.** Contacts displays the contact's data.
3. **Tap Add Photo.**
4. **Select an image using one of the following techniques:**
   - To assign an existing photo, tap All Photos and then use the Photos screen to locate and tap the photo you want to assign.
   - To take a new photo using your iPhone camera, tap the Camera icon, take the photo, move and scale the photo as needed, and then tap Use Photo.
   - To assign an animated Emoji, tap a character in the Animoji section, put on your favorite facial expression, and then press the Shutter button.
5. **Tap Done.** Contacts saves your work and returns you to the Contacts screen.

Creating a custom label

When you fill out contact data, your iPhone insists that you apply a label to each tidbit, such as home, work, and mobile. If none of the predefined labels fits, you can always just slap on the generic *other* label. However, this seems so, well, dull. If you've got a phone number or address that you can't shoehorn into any of the prefab labels, get creative and make one up. Here's how:

1. **With the contact's data open for editing, tap the label beside the field you want to work in.** The Label screen appears.
2. **Tap Add Custom Label.** Scroll to the bottom of the screen to see this command. The Custom Label screen appears.
3. **Type the custom label.**
4. **Tap Done.** Contacts returns you to the screen for the field you were editing and applies the new label.

Conveniently, you can apply your custom label to any type of contact data. For example, if you create a label named college, you can apply that label to a phone number, email address, web address, or physical address.

Managing contacts with Siri voice commands

The Siri voice recognition app enables you to locate and query your contacts using simple voice commands. To get started, tap and hold the Home button (or press and hold the Mic button of the iPhone headphones, or the equivalent button on a Bluetooth headset) until Siri appears.

To display one or more contacts, use the following techniques within Siri:

- **Displaying a specific contact.** Say "Show (or Display or Find) *first last*," where *first* and *last* are the person's first and last names as given in the Contacts list; you can also just say the person's name. If the contact is a business, say "Show (or Display or Find) *company*," where *company* is the business name as given in your Contacts list; you can also just say the company name.
- **Displaying a contact who has a relationship with you.** Say "Show (or Display or Find) *relationship*," where *relationship* is the connection you've defined (such as sister or father).
- **Displaying a contact with a unique first name.** Say "Show (or Display or Find) *first*," where *first* is the person's first name as given in your Contacts list.
- **Displaying multiple contacts who have some information in common.** Say "Find people *criteria*," where *criteria* defines the common data. Examples: "Find people named Stevens" or "Find people who live in New York."

To query your contacts, you use the following general syntax:

Question contact info?

Here, *question* can be "What is" (for general data), "When is" for dates, or "Who is" (for people); *contact* specifies the name (or relationship) of the contact; and *info* specifies the type of data you want to retrieve (such as "birthday" or "home phone number"). Here are some examples:

- "What is Alex Blandman's mobile phone number?"
- "When is my sister's anniversary?"
- "What is David Cutrere's address?"
- "Who is Kyra's husband?"

Tracking Your Events

When you meet someone and ask, "How are you?" the most common reply these days is a short one: "Busy!" We're all as busy as can be these days, and that places-to-go, people-to-see feeling is everywhere. That's all the more reason to keep your affairs in order, and that includes your appointments. Your iPhone comes with a Calendar app that you can use to create items called *events,* which represent your appointments, vacations, trips, meetings, and anything else that can be scheduled. Calendar acts as a kind of electronic personal assistant, leaving your brain free to concentrate on more important things.

Adding an event to your calendar

Adding a basic event to your calendar takes just a few steps, as shown here:

1. **In the Home screen, tap the Calendar icon.** The Calendar app appears.
2. **Using the week calendar near the top of the screen, scroll to the date on which the event occurs and then tap to select it.** If the event happens sometime in the future, tap the current month in the upper-left corner of the screen, scroll to the date, and then tap it.
3. **Tap the New Event (+) button at the top-right corner of the screen.** The New Event screen appears, as shown in Figure 8.2.
4. **The cursor starts off in the Title box, so enter a title for the event.**
5. **Tap the Location box, type the location of the event, and then either tap the location if it appears in the search results or tap Done.**
6. **Tap Starts and then use the scroll wheels to set the date and time that your event begins.**

8.2 Use the New Event screen to create your event.

7. **Tap Ends and then use the scroll wheels to set the date and time that your event finishes.**
8. **If you have multiple calendars, tap Calendar, and then tap the one in which you want this event to appear.**
9. **Tap Add.** The Calendar app adds the event to the calendar.

When you add an event in Calendar, the Month view displays a dot underneath the day as a visual reminder that you have something going on that day. Tap the day and Calendar displays a list of all the events you have scheduled. If you have multiple calendars and you want to see all your events, tap Calendars, tap Show All Calendars, and then tap Done.

Editing an existing event

After you've scheduled an event, the event details might change: a new time, a new location, and so on. Whatever the change, you need to edit the event to keep your schedule accurate. Here are the steps to follow to edit an existing event:

1. **In the Home screen, tap the Calendar icon.** The Calendar app appears.
2. **Tap the date that contains the event you want to edit.**
3. **Tap the event.** You can do this in either Month or Day view. Calendar displays the event info.
4. **Tap Edit.** Your iPhone displays the event data in the Edit screen.
5. **Make your changes to the event.**
6. **Tap Done.** Your iPhone saves your changes and returns you to the event details.

Setting up a repeating event

One of the truly great timesavers in Calendar is the repeat feature. It enables you to set up a single event and then get Calendar to automatically repeat it at a regular interval. For example, if you set up an event for a Friday, you can also set Calendar to automatically repeat it every Friday. You can continue repeating events indefinitely or end them on a specific date. Follow these steps to configure an existing event to repeat:

1. **In Calendar, tap the date that contains the event you want to edit.**
2. **Tap the event.** Calendar opens the event info.
3. **Tap Edit.** Calendar displays the event data in the Edit screen.
4. **Tap Repeat.** The Repeat screen appears.

5. **Tap the repeat interval you want to use.** Calendar selects the interval and returns you to the Edit screen.
6. **Tap End Repeat.** The End Repeat screen appears.
7. **You have two choices here (either way, tap Edit Event to return to the Edit screen when you're done):**
   - **Set the event to stop repeating on a particular day.** Tap On Date and then use the scroll wheels to set the day, month, and year that you want the final event to occur.
   - **Set the event to repeat indefinitely.** Tap Never.
8. **Tap Done.** Calendar saves the repeat data and returns you to the event details.

Converting an event to an all-day event

Some events don't really have specific times that you can pin down. These include birthdays, anniversaries, sales meetings, trade shows, conferences, and vacations. What all these types of events have in common is that they last all day: in the case of birthdays and anniversaries, literally so; in the case of trade shows and the like, "all day" refers to the entire workday.

To handle these scenarios, you can configure them as *all-day events*. Calendar clears them from the regular schedule and displays the event separately near the top of the Day view. Here are the steps to follow:

1. **In Calendar, tap the date that contains the event you want to edit.**
2. **Tap the event.** Calendar opens the event info.
3. **Tap Edit.** Calendar switches to the Edit screen.
4. **Tap the All-day switch to On.**
5. **Tap Done.** Calendar saves the event and returns you to the event details.

Adding an alert to an event

One of the truly useful secrets of stress-free productivity in the modern world is what I call the set-it-and-forget-it school of scheduling. That is, you set up an event electronically and then get the same technology to remind you when the event occurs. That way, your mind doesn't have to waste energy fretting about missing the event because you know your technology has your back.

With your iPhone, the technology of choice for doing this is Calendar and its alert feature. When you add an alert to an event, Calendar automatically displays a reminder of the event, which is a Notification Center banner that pops up on the screen. You can choose when the alert triggers (such as a specified number of minutes, hours, or days before the event), and you can even set up a second alert just to be on the safe side.

Caution

If you flick the Ring/Silent switch on the side of the iPhone to the Silent setting, remember that you won't hear the Calendar alert chirps. When the alert runs, your iPhone still vibrates and you still see the alert message on-screen.

Follow these steps to set an alert for an event:

1. **In Calendar, tap the date that contains the event you want to edit.**
2. **Tap the event.** Calendar opens the event info.
3. **Tap Edit.** Calendar displays the event data in the Edit screen.

Genius

You can save yourself some time by setting the default alert time for different types of events. Tap Settings in the Home screen, and then tap Mail, Contacts, Calendars. In the Calendars section, tap Default Alert Times, tap the type of alert you want to configure (Birthdays, Events, or All-Day Events), and then tap the default alert interval.

4. **Tap Alert.** The Alert screen appears, as shown in Figure 8.3.
5. **Tap the number of minutes, hours, or days before the event you want to see the alert.** If you're editing an all-day event, you can set the alert at 9 a.m. on the day of the event, or one day before, two days before, or a week before the event.
6. **To set up a backup alert, tap Second Alert.** Tap the number of minutes, hours, or days before the event you want to see the second alert, and then tap Done.
7. **Tap Done.** Calendar saves your alert choices and returns you to the event details.

Genius

You can disable the alert chirps if you find them annoying. On the Home screen, tap Settings, tap Sounds & Haptics, tap Calendar Alerts, and then tap None.

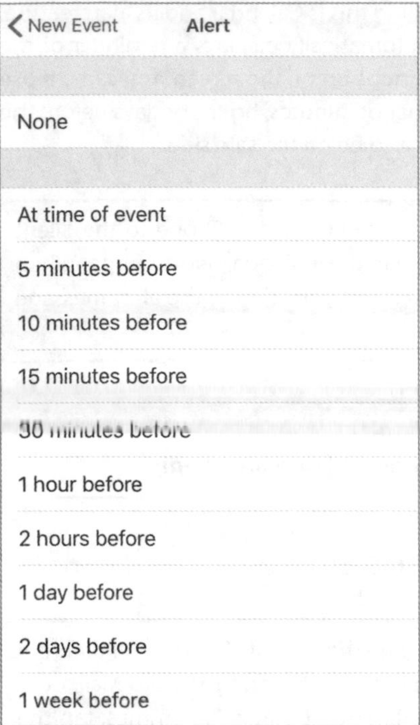

8.3 Use the Alert screen to tell Calendar when to remind you about your event.

Controlling events with Siri voice commands

Siri offers a number of voice commands for creating, editing, and querying your events.

To get Siri to schedule an event, you use the following general syntax:

Schedule what with *who* at *when*.

Here, *schedule* can be any of the following:

- "Schedule"
- "Meet"
- "Set up a meeting"
- "New appointment"

The *what* part of the command (which is optional) determines the topic of the event, so it could be something like "lunch" or "budget review" or "dentist"; you can also precede this part with "about" (for example, "about expenses"). The *who* part of the command specifies the person you're meeting with, if anyone, so it can be a contact name or a relationship (such as "my husband" or "Dad"). The *when* part of the command sets the time and date of the event; the time portion can be a specific time such as "3" (meaning 3 p.m.) or "8 a.m." or "noon"; the date portion can be "today" or "tomorrow," a day in the current week (such as "Tuesday" or "Friday"), a relative day (such as "next Monday"), or a specific date (such as "August 23rd").

Here are some examples:

- "Schedule lunch with Karen tomorrow at noon."
- "Meet with my sister Friday at 4."
- "Set up a meeting about budgeting next Tuesday at 10 a.m."
- "New appointment with Sarah Currid on March 15 at 2:30."

You can also use Siri to modify existing events. For example, you can change the event time by using the verbs "Reschedule" or "Move":

- "Reschedule my meeting with Sarah Currid to 3:30."
- "Move my noon appointment to 1:30."

You can also use the verb "Add" to include another person in a meeting, and the verb "Cancel" to remove a meeting from your schedule:

- "Add Charles Aster to the budgeting meeting."
- "Cancel my lunch with Karen."

Finally, you can query your events to see what's coming up. Here are some examples:

- "When is my next appointment?"
- "When is my meeting with Sarah Currid?"
- "What is on my Calendar tomorrow?"
- "What does the rest of my day look like?"

Creating Reminders

Our days are littered with tasks that could be called *subevents*. These are things that need to be done at a certain point during your day but don't rise to the level of full-fledged events: returning a call, taking the laundry out of the dryer, turning off the sprinkler. If you need to be reminded to perform such a subevent, it seems like overkill to crank out an event using the Calendar app.

Fortunately, iOS offers a better solution: the Reminders app. You use this app to create *reminders,* which are simple nudges that tell you to do something, to be somewhere, or whatever. These nudges come in the form of Notification Center banners that appear on your screen at a time you specify or when your iPhone reaches a particular location.

Setting a reminder for a specific time

Here are the steps to follow to set up a reminder that alerts you at a specific time:

1. **On the iPhone Home screen, tap Reminders.** The Reminders app appears.
2. **Tap the list you want to use to store the reminder.** If you don't see your lists, tap Lists in the upper-left corner of the screen.
3. **Tap New Reminder at the bottom of the screen.** The Reminders app creates a new reminder.
4. **Type the reminder text and then tap the More Info icon (the *i*) that appears on the right side of the new reminder.** The Details screen appears, as shown in Figure 8.4.

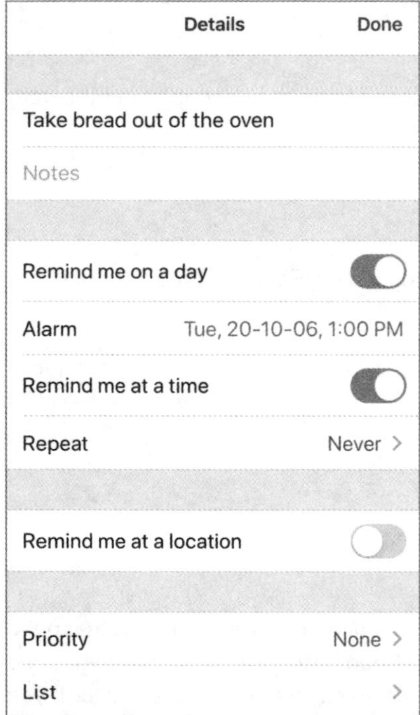

8.4 Tap More Info to see the full Details screen options.

5. **Tap the Date switch to On and then use the calendar that appears to set the date of the reminder.**
6. **Tap the Time switch to On and then use the controls that appear to set the time of the reminder.**

Genius

Actually, setting a specific reminder time is optional. If you leave the Time switch Off, Reminders creates an *all-day* reminder that appears at 9 a.m. on the day you select. You can change the default all-day reminder time by opening the Settings app, tapping Reminders, and then tapping the time in the All-Day Reminders section.

7. **Use the Repeat setting to set up a repeat interval for the reminder.**
8. **Use the Priority setting to assign a priority to the reminder: None, Low, Medium, or High.**
9. **Use the Notes text box to add some background text or other information about the reminder.**
10. **Tap Done.** Reminders saves the reminder.

Setting a reminder for a specific location

Getting an alert at a specific time is the standard way of working with reminders, but the Reminders app supports a second type of criterion: location. That is, when you specify a particular location for a reminder, the app sets up a *geo-fence* — a kind of virtual border — around that location. When your iPhone crosses that geo-fence, the associated reminder appears on your screen. So, for example, if you're on your way to a meeting with a client, you could create a reminder that includes notes about the meeting or the client, and then specify the meeting location as the criterion. Here's how it works:

1. **On the iPhone Home screen, tap Reminders.** The Reminders app appears.
2. **Tap the list you want to use to store the reminder.** If an existing list is displayed and you want to choose another, tap Lists in the upper-left corner of the screen and then tap the list you want to use.
3. **Tap New Reminder.** The Reminders app creates a new reminder.
4. **Type the reminder text and then tap the More Info icon (the *i*) that appears on the right side of the new reminder.** The Details screen appears.

5. **Tap the Location switch to On.** If your iPhone asks whether the Reminders app can use your location, tap Allow.
6. **Tap Custom.** The Location screen appears.
7. **Use the Search box to specify the address of the location you want to use, and then tap the location when it appears in the search results.** Alternatively, you can tap Current Location to use your present whereabouts.
8. **To have the reminder appear when your iPhone first comes within range of the location, tap Arriving.** If you prefer to see the reminder when your iPhone goes out of range of the location, tap Leaving, instead.

Genius

If you don't see the Arriving and Leaving buttons, it means the keyboard is on top of them. Swipe up on an empty part of the screen to dismiss the keyboard.

9. **Tap Details and then follow Steps 7 to 10 from the previous section to fill in the reminder details.**

Creating a new list

The Reminders app comes with three preset lists that you can use: Reminders, Home, and Work. The default is Reminders, but you can also select a different list if it's more suitable or if you want to keep your personal and business reminders separate. If none of these three prefab lists is exactly right for your needs, feel free to create your own list by following these steps:

1. **If the Reminders app is currently displaying a list, tap Lists in the upper-left corner.** The Reminders app displays the Lists screen.
2. **Tap Add List at the bottom of the screen.**
3. **Tap the name of your list.**
4. **Tap Done.** The Reminders app adds the list.

Completing a reminder

When a reminder is complete, you don't want it lingering in the Reminders list (or whatever list it's in), cluttering the screen and making it hard to look through your remaining reminders. To avoid that, once the reminder is done, tap the radio button beside it. This tells Reminders that the reminder is complete, and the app immediately moves it to the Completed list.

Deleting a reminder

If you no longer need a reminder, it's a good idea to delete it to keep your reminder lists neat and tidy. To delete a reminder, follow these steps:

1. **In the Reminder app, tap the list that contains the reminder you want to delete.** The Reminders app displays the list's reminders.
2. **Swipe left on the reminder you want to delete.** Reminders displays a Delete button to the right of the reminder.
3. **Tap Delete.** Reminders deletes the reminder.

Genius

If you're in a hurry, you can delete a reminder in a single step by sliding a finger left along the reminder all the way to the left edge of the screen.

Setting the default Reminders list

The default list is the one that Reminders uses when you don't specify a particular list when you create a reminder. If you have a particular list you'd prefer to use as the default, follow these steps to set it:

1. **On the Home screen, tap Settings.** The Settings app appears.
2. **Tap Reminders.** The Reminders screen appears.
3. **Tap Default List.** The Default List screen appears.
4. **Tap the list you want to use as the default.**

Setting reminders with Siri voice commands

You can also create reminders via voice using the Siri app. Time-based reminders use the following general syntax:

Remind me to *action* at *when*.

Here, *action* is the task you want to be reminded to perform, and *when* is the date and time you want to be reminded (as described earlier in the chapter when I discuss creating calendar events using Siri). Here are some examples:

- "Remind me to call my wife at 5."
- "Remind me to pick up Greg at the airport tomorrow at noon."
- "Remind me to bring lunch."

Location-based reminders use the following general syntax:

Remind me to *action* when I *location*.

Again, *action* is the task you want to be reminded to perform; *location* is the place around which you want the geo-fence set up (including either "get to" or "leave," depending on whether you want to be reminded coming or going). Here are some examples:

- "Remind me to pick up milk when I leave here."
- "Remind me to call my husband when I get to LaGuardia Airport."
- "Remind me to call my sister when I get home."
- "Remind me to grab my sample case when I arrive at Acme Limited."

For the last of these, you can assume that "Acme Limited" is a company name defined (with an address) in your Contacts list.

How Do I Use My iPhone to Navigate My World?

1 2 3 4 5 6 7 8 9 10 11

Dedicated GPS devices have become gasp-inducingly popular over the past few years because it's not easy finding your way around in a strange city or an unfamiliar part of town. The old way — deciphering hastily scribbled directions or scratching your head over a possibly out-of-date map — was just too hard and error prone, so having a device tell you where to go (so to speak) was a no-brainer. However, dedicated devices, whether they're music players, e-book readers, or GPS receivers, are going the way of the dodo. They're being replaced by multifunction devices that can play music, read books, and display maps. In this chapter, you take advantage of the multifunction prowess of your iPhone to learn about the amazingly useful Maps app and other iOS location services.

Finding Your Way with Maps and GPS

When you're out in the real world trying to navigate your way between the proverbial points A and B, the questions often come thick and fast: "Where am I now?" "Which turn do I take?" "What's the traffic like on the highway?" "Can I even get there from here?" Fortunately, the answers to those and similar questions are now just a few finger taps away. That's because your iPhone comes loaded not only with a way-cool Maps app but also a GPS receiver. Now your iPhone knows exactly where it is (and so, by extension, do you), and it can help you get where you want to go.

To get the Maps app on the job, tap the Maps icon on the iPhone Home screen. Figure 9.1 shows the initial Maps screen. (If you see a dialog letting you know that Maps would like to use your current location, say "Out of course!" and tap Allow While Using App.)

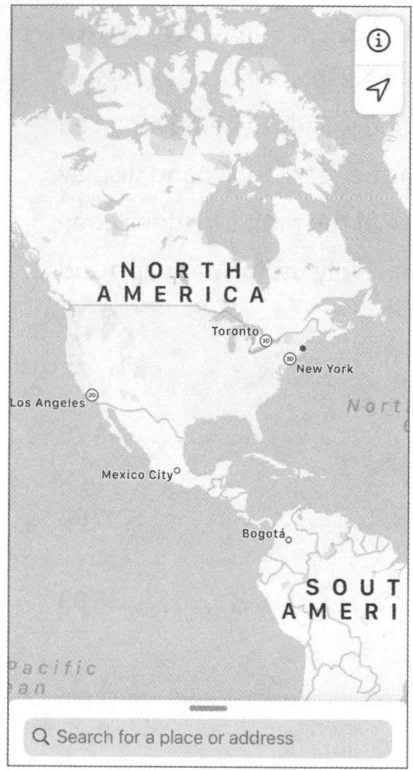

9.1 Use the Maps app to navigate your world.

Searching for a destination

When you want to locate a destination using Maps, the most straightforward method is to search for it:

1. **Tap inside the Search for a Place or Address box.**
2. **Type the name, address, or a keyword or phrase that describes your destination.**
3. **In the on-screen keyboard, tap Search.** Maps locates the destination, moves the map to that area, and displays the location on the map, as shown in Figure 9.2.

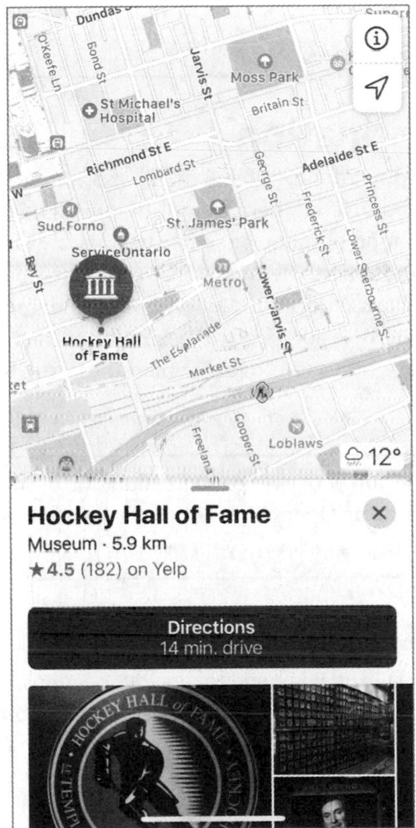

9.2 When you search for a destination, Maps marks the location on the map.

Now that you have your destination pinpointed, you can read the map to find your way by looking for street names, local landmarks, nearby major intersections, and so on. (You also can use the Maps app to get specific directions; I show you how that works later in this chapter.) The map is also rotatable, so, for example, if you're physically facing east, you can rotate the map so that it also faces east and you can more easily get your bearings. To rotate the map, place two fingers on the screen and rotate either clockwise or counterclockwise.

Genius

You can save time using Maps by adding common locations to the Favorites list, which you can display by swiping up on the bar above the Search for a Place or Address box. Tap Add, search for and select the location, and then tap Done. You can also tap the Home and Work icons to add those locations to Favorites.

Getting info about a destination

Knowing where a destination is located is a good thing, but you might also want to find out more about that destination. Maps has you covered there, as well, because it not only provides you with general info such as a phone number, street address, and web site address, but it also ties into Yelp, a service that offers user-generated content — particularly ratings, reviews, and photos — of millions of locations around the world. Tap the destination (or drag up the destination name that appears at the bottom of the Maps screen), and, as you can see in Figure 9.3, Maps offers tons of data about the destination, including basic info, reviews, and photos.

Genius

If you have a Yelp account, you can add your own content about the destination. In the What People Say section, tap Open Yelp to open the Yelp app and see all the reviews. Tap Add (+) to post a review of your own.

Displaying your current location

When you arrive at an unfamiliar shopping mall and you need to get your bearings, your first instinct might be to seek out the nearest mall map and look for the inevitable *You are here* marker. This gives you a sense of your current location with respect to the rest of the mall, so locating Pottery Barn shouldn't be all that hard.

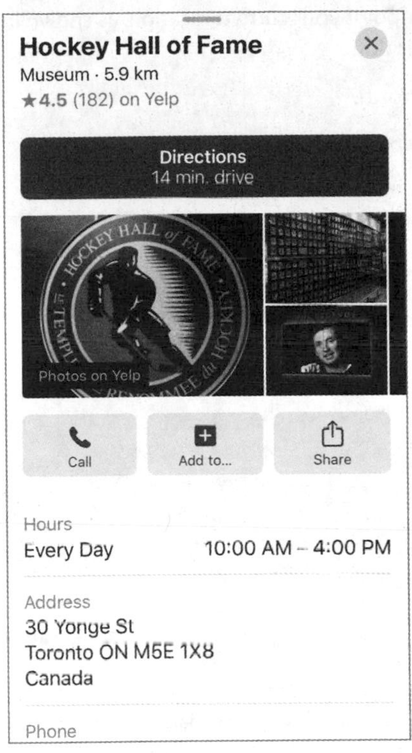

9.3 Maps gives you access to information about the destination as well as Yelp ratings, reviews, and photos.

When you arrive at an unfamiliar part of town or a new city, have you ever wished you had something that could provide you with that same *You are here* reference point? If so, you're in luck because you have exactly that waiting for you right in your iPhone. Tap the Tracking icon in the upper-right corner of the screen, as pointed out in Figure 9.4. (If this is the first time you've used the Tracking icon, Maps asks for permission to use your current location, so be sure to tap Allow While Using App.)

That's it! Your iPhone examines GPS coordinates, Wi-Fi hotspots, and nearby cellular towers to plot your current position. When it completes the necessary processing and triangulating, your iPhone displays a map of your current city, zooms in on your current area, and then adds a blue dot to the map to pinpoint your current location, as shown in Figure 9.4. Here are two things to note about this dot:

- The little arrow attached to the dot points north.
- To orient your map so that north is at the top of the screen, tap the Tracking icon again.

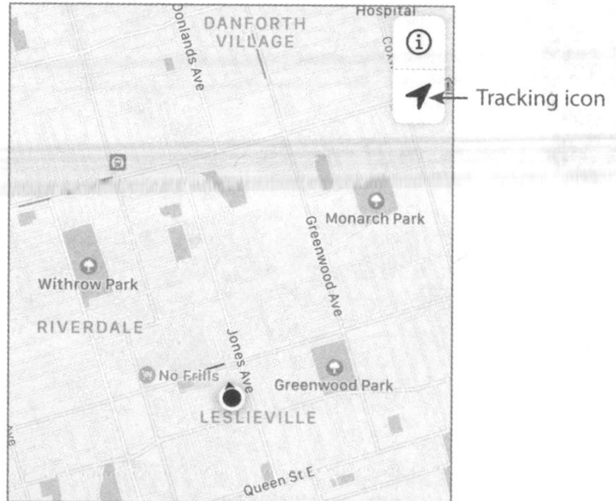

9.4 Tap the Tracking icon to see your precise location as a blue dot on a map.

Seeing what's near you

Knowing where you are is a good thing, but it's even better to know what's nearby. For example, suppose you're in a new city and you're dying for a cup of coffee. You could tap Search in the menu bar, tap the Search box, type something like coffee (or perhaps café or espresso, depending on what you're looking for), and then tap Search. That works, but you might notice something interesting: When you tap inside the Search box, Maps displays icons for a bunch of categories, including Restaurants, Gas Stations, Hospitals, and Parking, as shown in Figure 9.5. Tap one of these icons (such as Coffee Shops) and Maps drops a bunch of pins that correspond to nearby locations that match the subcategory you tapped. Tap a pin to see the location's name, phone number, address, and other info.

Displaying a map of a contact's location

In the old days (that is, a few years ago), if you had a contact located in an unfamiliar part of town or even in another city altogether, visiting that person required a phone call or email asking for directions. You'd then write down the instructions, get written directions via email, or perhaps even get a crudely drawn map faxed to you. Those days, fortunately, are long gone thanks to myriad online resources that can show you where a particular address is located and even give you driving directions to get there from here (wherever *here* may be).

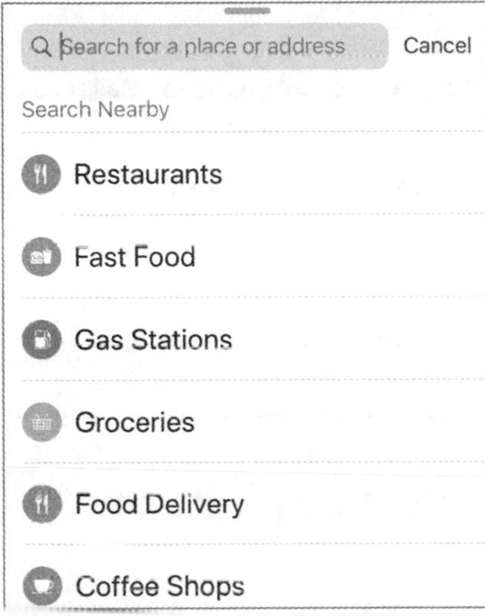

9.5 Tap inside the Search box to see these category icons.

Even better, your iPhone takes it one step further and integrates with Maps to generate a map of a contact's location based on the person's contact address. So as long as you've tapped in (or synced) a contact's physical address, you can see where the person is located on the map.

To display a map of a contact's location, follow these steps:

1. **On the Home screen, tap the Contacts icon.** The Contacts app appears.
2. **Tap the contact you want to map.** Your iPhone displays the contact's data.
3. **Tap the address you want to view.** Your iPhone switches to the Maps app and drops a pushpin on the contact's location.

Mapping an address from an email

Addresses show up in all kinds of email messages these days. Most commonly, folks include their work or home addresses in their email signatures at the bottom of each message. Similarly, if the email is an invitation, your correspondent almost certainly includes the address for the event somewhere in the message.

If you need to know where an address is located, you might think that you need to copy the address from the message and then paste it into the Maps app. Sure, that works, but it's way too much effort! Instead, just do this:

1. **In the Mail app, display the message that includes the address.**
2. **Tap and hold on the address in the message to display a list of actions.** If the address is displayed as a link (that is, underlined in a blue font), it means Mail recognizes it as an address, so you can just tap the address and skip the next step.
3. **Tap Open in Maps.** The Maps app opens and drops a pushpin on the address.

Note

Instead of tapping Open in Maps, you can tap Get Directions to open Maps and display directions to the location. You learn more about getting directions to a location later in this chapter.

Specifying a location when you don't know the exact address

Sometimes you have only a vague notion of where you want to go. In a new city, for example, you might decide to head downtown and then see whether there are any good coffee shops or restaurants. That's fine, but how do you get downtown from your hotel in the suburbs? Your iPhone can give you directions, but it needs to know the endpoint of your journey, and that's precisely the information you don't have. Sounds like a conundrum, for sure, but there's a way to work around it. You can drop a pin on the map in the approximate area where you want to go. The Maps app can then give you directions to the dropped pin.

Here are the steps to follow to drop a pin on a map:

1. **In the Maps app, display a map of the city you want to work with:**
   - If you're in the city now, tap the Tracking icon in the lower-left corner of the screen.
   - If you're not in the city, tap Search, tap the Search box, type the name of the city (and perhaps also the name of the state or province), and then tap the Search button.
2. **Use finger flicks to pan the map to the approximate location you want to use as your destination.**
3. **Tap and hold on the destination location.** The Maps app drops a pin named Marked Location that you can use when you ask the iPhone for directions (as described next).

Getting directions to a location

"Can I get there from here?" To answer that age-old question, the Maps app not only can show you a route to the destination but also provide you with the distance and time it should take and give you street-by-street, turn-by-turn instructions, whether you're driving, walking, or taking transit. It's one of the sweetest features of your iPhone, and it works like so:

1. **Use the Maps app to add a pushpin for your journey's destination.** Use whatever method works best for you: the Contacts list, a name or address search, or a marked location.
2. **Tap Directions.** As shown in Figure 9.6, Maps displays several routes, all of which assume you want to leave from your current location and that you want to drive. If those assumptions apply, skip to Step 4.

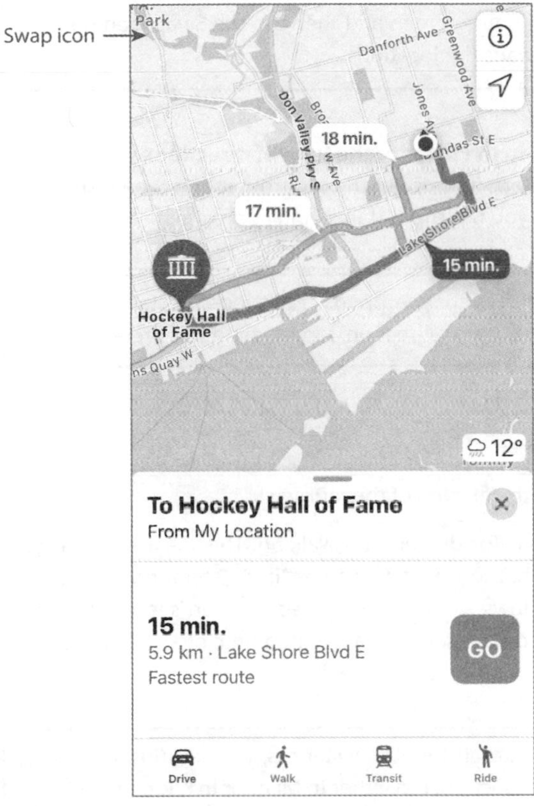

9.6 Maps initially displays several driving routes originating from your current location.

3. **If you want to use a starting point other than your current location, follow these substeps:**

   a. **Tap My Location.** Maps opens the Change Route screen, shown in Figure 9.7.

   b. **Select or enter a new location in the From box.**

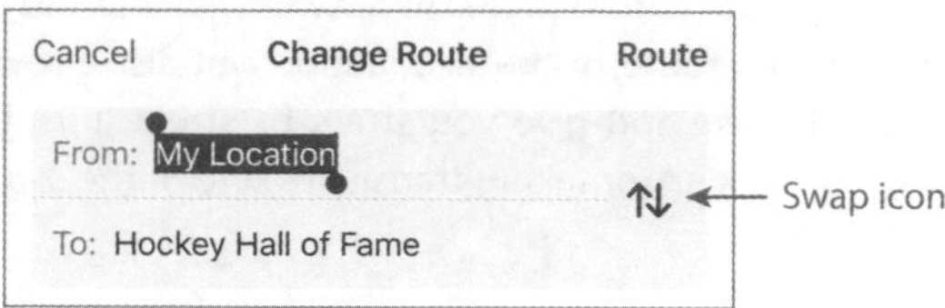

9.7 Use the Change Route screen to change your starting location.

   c. **Tap Route.** Maps returns you to the routes.

Genius

Instead of getting directions to the destination, you might need directions *from* the destination. No sweat. When you map the destination, tap My Location to open the Change Route screen and then tap the Swap icon pointed out in Figure 9.7. Maps swaps the locations.

4. **At the bottom of the screen, tap the icon for the type of directions you want: Drive, Walk, Transit, or Ride.** Maps figures out the best routes and then displays them on the map; it also shows you the trip distance and approximate time.

Genius

To set your default transportation type, open the Settings app, tap Maps, and then, in the Preferred Type of Travel section, tap the type you prefer.

5. **Tap the route you prefer to take.**

6. **Tap Go.** The Maps app displays the first leg of the journey.

Maps features turn-by-turn directions for driving and walking. This means that as you approach each turn, Siri tells you what to do next, such as "In 400 feet, turn right onto Main Street." The Maps app also follows along the route, so you can see where you're going and what turn is coming up. You can see your estimated time of arrival, remaining travel time, and distance remaining by tapping the screen.

Note

To switch between standard and metric distances, tap Settings, tap Maps, and then, in the Distances section, tap either In Miles or In Kilometers.

Getting more info about a location

The Maps apps offers quite a few more features, most of which you'll rarely use. However, I think you'll be glad to know about the following ways to get more information about a location:

- **Traffic info.** Maps displays an orange dotted line to indicate traffic slowdowns and shows a red dashed line to indicate heavy traffic. To make sure you see all this, tap Maps Settings (pointed out in Figure 9.8) and then tap the Traffic switch to On.
- **Roadwork info.** In major cities, Maps displays a Roadwork icon at locations where there is road construction. Tap the icon to see more information, as shown in Figure 9.8.

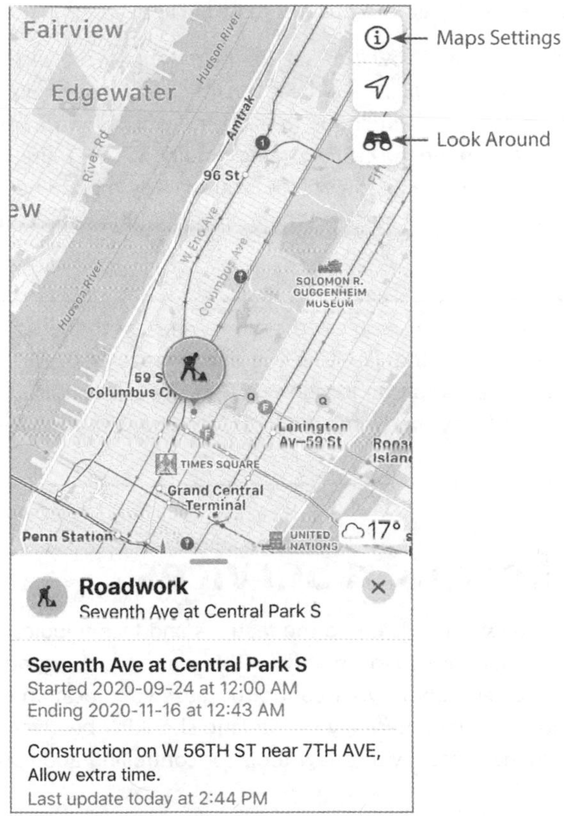

9.8 For many metropolitan areas, Maps displays Roadwork icons to indicate road construction sites.

- **Transit info.** Maps offers a Transit layer that shows information about transit stops and lines. To see this layer, tap Maps Settings (pointed out in Figure 9.8) and then tap Transit.
- **Street-level imagery.** To see interactive, high-resolution photography of an area, tap Look Around (pointed out in Figure 9.8). Note that Apple is currently rolling out this feature to select cities in the United States, so if you don't see the Look Around icon, it means this feature isn't available for the current location.

Controlling Maps with Siri voice commands

You can use the Siri voice-activated assistant to control Maps with straightforward voice commands. You can display a location, get directions, and even display traffic information. Tap and hold the Home button (or press and hold the Mic button of the iPhone headphones, or the equivalent button on a Bluetooth headset) until Siri appears.

To display a location in Maps via Siri, say "Show *location*" (or "Map *location*" or "Find *location*" or "Where is *location*?"), where *location* is an address, a name, or a Maps bookmark. Similarly, to get directions from Siri, say "Directions to *location*," where *location* is an address, name, or a Maps bookmark. To see the current traffic conditions, say "Traffic *location*," where *location* can be a specific place or someplace local, such as "around here" or "nearby." To get your current location, you can say "Where am I?" or "Show my current location."

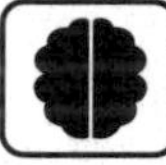

Genius

Siri generally ignores extra terms you say that aren't relevant to the task at hand. So, you can say something like "Give me directions to Hoover Dam" and Siri won't miss a beat. Also, the location you specify can be based on Contacts data, such as "Show my wife's work" or "Directions to my sister's home."

Configuring Location Services

On your iPhone, the term *location services* refers to the features and technologies that provide apps and system tools with access to location data. This is a handy thing, but it's also something that you need to keep under your control because your location data, particularly your current location, is fundamentally private and shouldn't be given out willy-nilly. Fortunately, your iPhone comes with a few tools for controlling and configuring location services.

Turning off location services

The next couple of sections show you how to turn off location services for individual apps as well as individual system services. That fine-grained control is the best way to handle location services, but there may be times when you prefer a broader approach that turns off location services altogether. For example, if you're heading to a secret rendezvous (how exciting!) and you're bringing your iPhone with you, you might feel more comfortable knowing that no app or service on your iPhone is tracking your whereabouts. On a more mundane level, location services use up battery power, so if your iPhone is getting low or if you just want to maximize the battery (for a long bus ride, for example), then turning off location services completely will help.

Follow these steps to turn off all location services on your iPhone:

1. **On the Home screen, tap Settings.** The Settings app appears.
2. **Tap Privacy.** The Privacy settings appear.
3. **Tap Location Services.** The Location Services settings appear.
4. **Tap the Location Services switch to the Off position.** If you have Find My iPhone activated (see Chapter 2), your iPhone asks you to confirm.
5. **Tap Turn Off.** Your iPhone shuts off all location services.

Controlling app access to GPS

When you open an app that comes with a GPS component, the app displays a dialog like the one shown in Figure 9.9 to ask your permission to use the GPS hardware in your iPhone to determine your current location:

- **Allow While Using App.** Tap this option to allow the app to access your location only while you use the app. Once you exit the app, it can no longer access your location.
- **Allow Once.** Tap this option to give the app one-time permission to use your location. The next time you start the app, it will ask for your permission again.
- **Don't Allow.** Tap this option if you think that your current location is none of the app's business.

9.9 When you first launch a GPS-aware app, it asks your permission to access your current location while you use the app.

Whatever type of permission you choose, after you make your decision, you might change your mind. For example, if you deny your location to an app, that app might lack some crucial functionality. Similarly, if you allow an app to use your location, you might have second thoughts about compromising your privacy.

Whatever the reason, you can control an app's access to GPS by following these steps:

1. **In your Home screen, tap Settings.** The Settings app appears.
2. **Tap Privacy.** The Privacy settings appear.
3. **Tap Location Services.** The Location Services screen appears.
4. **Tap the app you want to configure.**
5. **Tap one of the following:**
   - **Never.** Tap this setting to deny your current location to the app.
   - **Ask Next Time.** Tap this setting to force the app to ask your permission the next time you launch the app.
   - **While Using the App.** Tap this setting to give the app permission to use your location only while you use the app.
   - **Always.** Tap this setting (which is available only for certain apps) to give the app access to your location even when you're not using the app.

Enabling or disabling system location services

Your iPhone also provides location services to various internal system services that perform tasks, such as calibrating the iPhone compass, setting the time zone, and serving up iAds that change depending on location data. If you don't want your iPhone providing any of these services, you can turn them off this way:

1. **On the Home screen, tap Settings.** The Settings app appears.
2. **Tap Privacy.** The Privacy screen appears.
3. **Tap Location Services.** The Location Services screen appears.
4. **Tap System Services.** The Settings app displays the System Services screen.
5. **For any system service to which you don't want to provide access to location data, tap its switch to Off.**

Sharing Map Data

If you want to show someone where you live, where you work, or where you want to meet, you could just send the address, but that's so last century. The more modern way is to send your friend a digital map that shows the location. With your iPhone this is a snap — you can send a map via email or text message or post a map on Twitter.

Here are the steps to follow:

1. **Use the Maps app to add a pushpin for the location you want to send.** Use whatever method works best for you: the Contacts list, an address search, or a marked location. If you want to send your current location, display it, and then tap the blue dot.

2. **Tap the location banner.** Maps displays the Location screen for the location.

3. **Tap Share.** Maps displays a list of ways to share the map.

4. **Tap the method you want to use to share the map.** The Maps app creates a new document (such as an email message, text message, tweet, or post) that includes a Maps link to the location.

5. **Fill in the rest of your message and then send it.**

Alternatively, if the other person is nearby (that is, within 30 feet or so), you can use AirDrop to exchange the location wirelessly. Here's how it works:

1. **Use the Maps app to add a pushpin for the location you want to send.** Use whatever method works best for you: the Contacts list, an address search, or a marked location. If you want to send your current location, display it, and then tap the blue dot.

2. **Tap the location banner.** Maps displays the Location screen for the location.

3. **Tap Share.** Maps displays a list of ways to share the location.

4. **In the AirDrop section, tap the icon for the person with whom you want to share the location.** The other person sees a dialog asking for permission to share the location, and when she taps Accept, her version of Maps loads and displays the location.

How Do I Keep My Life in Sync with iCloud?

1 2 3 4 5 6 7 8 9 10 11

When you go online, you take your life along with you, of course, so your online world becomes a natural extension of your real world. However, just because it's online doesn't mean the digital version of your life is any less busy, chaotic, or complex than the rest of your life. The Apple iCloud service is designed to ease some of that chaos and complexity by automatically syncing your most important data — your email, contacts, calendars, photos, notes, and bookmarks. Although the syncing may be automatic, setting up is not, unfortunately. This chapter shows you what to do.

Understanding iCloud

These days, the primary source of online chaos and confusion is the ongoing proliferation of services and sites that demand your time and attention. What started with web-based email has grown to a web site, a blog, a photo-sharing site, online bookmarks, and perhaps a few social networking sites, just to consume those last few precious moments of leisure time. You might be sitting in a chair, but you're being run ragged anyway!

A great way to simplify your online life is to get a free iCloud account. You get a one-stop web shop that includes email, an address book, a calendar, and 5GB of online file storage. If you want more storage, you can get 50GB for $0.99 a month, 200GB for $2.99 a month, or 2TB for $9.99 a month (these prices are in U.S. dollars).

The web applications that make up iCloud — Mail, Contacts, Calendar, Photos, iCloud Drive, Find iPhone, Find Friends, Notes, Reminders, Pages, Numbers, and Keynote — are certainly useful and are surprisingly functional for online applications. However, the big news with iCloud is the "cloud" part of the name. This means that your data, particularly your email accounts, contacts, calendars, and bookmarks, is stored on a bunch of icloud.com networked servers that Apple collectively calls *the cloud*. When you log in to your iCloud account at icloud.com, you use the web applications to interact with that data.

That's pretty mundane stuff, right? What's revolutionary here is that you can let the cloud know about all the other devices in your life: your Mac, your home computer, your work PC, your notebook, your iPad, and, of course, your iPhone. If you sign in to your iCloud account and, say, add a new appointment, the cloud takes that appointment and immediately sends the data to all your devices. Fire up your Mac, open Calendar, and the appointment is there; switch to your Windows PC, click the Outlook Calendar folder, and the appointment is there; tap Calendar on your iPhone Home screen and, yup, the appointment is there, too.

This works if you change data on any of your devices. Move an email message to another folder on your Mac, and the same message is moved to the same folder on the other devices and on your iCloud account; modify a contact on your Windows PC, and the changes also propagate everywhere else. In each case, the new or changed data is sent to the cloud, which then sends the data to each device, usually in a matter of seconds.

Note

If you've used email, contacts, and calendars in a company that runs Microsoft Exchange Server, then you're no doubt used to push technology because Exchange has done that for a while through ActiveSync (a feature that your iPhone supports, by the way). iCloud push is a step up, however, because you don't need a behemoth corporate server to make it happen. Apple calls iCloud "Exchange for the rest of us."

With iCloud, you never have to worry about entering the same information into all your devices. With iCloud, you won't miss an important meeting because you forgot to enter it into the calendar on your work computer. With iCloud, you can never forget data when you're traveling because you have up-to-the-moment data with you at all times. iCloud practically organizes your life for you; all you have to do is show up.

Understanding iCloud System Support

iCloud promises to simplify your online life, but the first step to that simpler existence is to configure iCloud on all the devices that you want to keep in sync. The next few sections show you how to configure iCloud on various devices, but it's important to understand exactly what operating systems can do the iCloud thing. Here's a summary:

- **iOS.** iCloud works with any device running version 5.1.1 or newer of iOS. However, Apple recommends devices running at least iOS 14, which requires an iPhone 6s or newer, or iPadOS 14, which requires an iPad 5th generation or newer, an iPad Air 2nd generation or newer, or an iPad mini 4th generation or newer.
- **Mac.** Many iCloud features work with a minimum of OS X Lion (10.7.5), but Apple recommends running macOS Catalina (10.15) or newer. To access the iCloud web applications, you should be using Safari 9.1 or newer, Chrome 54 or newer, or Firefox 45 or newer.
- **Windows.** Any Windows 7, 8, or 10 version works with iCloud, but Apple recommends using the Windows 10 May 2019 Update or newer. To access the iCloud web applications, either you can use the Microsoft Edge browser that comes with Windows 10 or you can use Firefox 45 or newer, or Chrome 54 or newer. For push email, contacts, and calendars, you need Outlook 2010 or newer.

Configuring iCloud on Your iPhone

iCloud is designed particularly with the iPhone in mind because it's when you're on the town or on the road that you need data pushed to you. To ensure your iPhone works seamlessly with your iCloud data, you need to add your iCloud account and configure the iCloud sync settings on your iPhone.

Setting up your iCloud account on your iPhone

Start by setting up your iCloud account on your iPhone:

1. **On the Home screen, tap Settings.** Your iPhone opens the Settings app.
2. **Tap Mail.** The Mail screen appears.
3. **Tap Accounts.** The Accounts screen appears.
4. **Tap Add Account.** The Add Account screen appears.
5. **Tap the iCloud logo.** Your iPhone displays the iCloud screen, as shown in Figure 10.1.

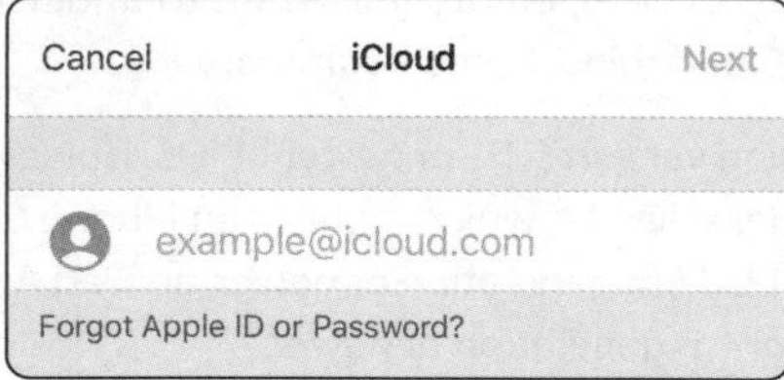

10.1 Use the iCloud screen to configure your iCloud account on your iPhone.

6. **Enter your iCloud email address and tap Next.** The password field appears.
7. **Enter your iCloud password and tap Next.** Your iPhone verifies the account info and then asks what type of data you want pushed to your iPhone, as shown in Figure 10.2.

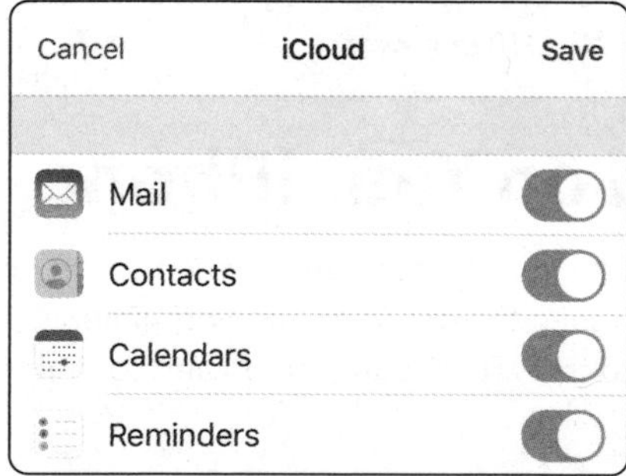

10.2 Use this iCloud screen to specify the types of data you want iCloud to push to your iPhone.

8. **If there are any data types you don't want pushed to your iPhone, tap the corresponding switch to Off.**
9. **Tap Save.** Your iPhone returns you to the Mail settings screen with your iCloud account added to the Accounts list.

Setting up iCloud synchronization on your iPhone

No matter where you are, iCloud ensures that your email messages, contacts, and calendars get pushed to your iPhone and remain fully synced with all your other devices. Your iPhone comes with this push feature turned on, but if you want to double-check this or if you want to turn off push to concentrate on something else, you can configure the setting by following these steps:

1. **In the Home Screen, tap Settings.** The Settings app appears.
2. **Tap your name, which appears at the top of the Settings screen.** The Apple ID screen appears.
3. **Tap iCloud.** Settings displays the iCloud screen, as shown in Figure 10.3.
4. **If there are any apps whose data you don't want pushed to your iPhone, tap the corresponding switch to Off in the Apps Using iCloud section.**

Setting up and using Family Sharing

iCloud offers Family Sharing, which enables up to six family members to share each other's content, including photos, calendars, and reminders. If purchases are made through the App Store, iTunes Store, or Book Store using a single credit card, then each family member also gets access to purchased apps, songs, movies, TV shows, and e-books.

Assuming you'll be the Family Organizer (that is, the person who'll be setting up and maintaining Family Sharing), follow these steps to get things started:

1. **Tap Settings to launch the Settings app.**
2. **Tap your name, which appears at the top of the Settings screen.** The Apple ID screen appears.
3. **Tap Set Up Family Sharing.** iCloud displays an overview of Family Sharing.
4. **Tap Start Sharing.** iCloud prompts you to invite other members of your family.

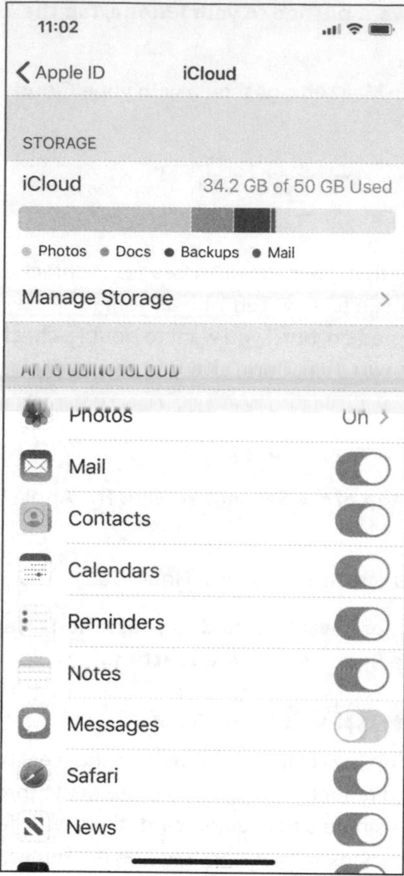

10.3 Use the iCloud screen to configure iCloud synchronization on your iPhone.

5. **Tap Invite Family Members.** iCloud creates a new text message that includes an invitation to join Family Sharing.
6. **Address the message to each family member you want to invite.**
7. **(Optional) Add your own message text below the invitation.**
8. **Tap Send.** iCloud sends the invitations.
9. **Tap Done.** Alternatively, you can tap Manage Family to open the Family Sharing screen, shown in Figure 10.4.

Note

You can get to the Family Sharing screen any time by opening Settings, tapping your name, and then tapping Family Sharing.

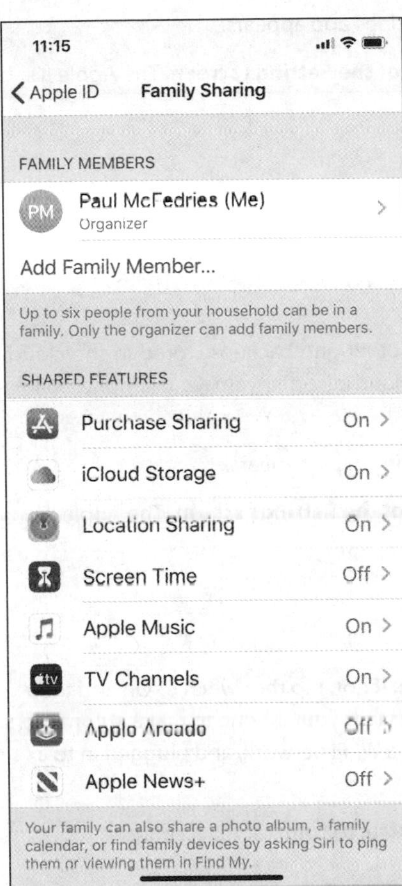

10.4 As the Family Organizer, you use this screen to add family members and specify what features are shared with your family members.

Setting up iCloud Keychain

A *keychain* is a master list of usernames and passwords that a system stores for easy access by an authorized user. iCloud Keychain is a special type of keychain that stores website passwords autogenerated by Safari. This means you don't have to remember these passwords because Safari can automatically retrieve them from your iCloud account. Even better, any other iOS device or Mac that uses the same iCloud account has access to the same keychain, so your web-site passwords also work on those devices.

Follow these steps to set up your iCloud Keychain on your iPhone:

1. **In the Home Screen, tap Settings.** The Settings app appears.
2. **Tap your name, which appears at the top of the Settings screen.** The Apple ID screen appears.
3. **Tap iCloud to open the iCloud settings.**
4. **Tap Keychain.**
5. **Tap the iCloud Keychain switch to On.**

Backing up your iPhone

If you have an iCloud account, you can have your iPhone backups stored in the cloud. To set this up, and to back up your data to iCloud directly from your iPhone, follow these steps:

1. **In the Home Screen, tap Settings.** The Settings app appears.
2. **Tap your name, which appears at the top of the Settings screen.** The Apple ID screen appears.
3. **Tap iCloud to open the iCloud settings.**
4. **Tap Backup.**
5. **Check that the iCloud Backup switch is On.** If not, tap the switch to On and then tap OK when iCloud confirms the setting. This tells your iPhone to make automatic backups whenever it is locked, connected to a Wi-Fi network, and plugged in to a power source.
6. **Tap Back Up Now.** Your iPhone backs up its data to your iCloud account.

Managing your iCloud storage

I mention earlier that your iCloud account comes with 5GB of storage free. That storage is used for your iCloud Photo Library, device backups, email, and app documents and data. If you find that you're running low on storage space, follow these steps to remove data and free up some cloud headroom:

1. **In the Home Screen, tap Settings.** The Settings app appears.
2. **Tap your name, which appears at the top of the Settings screen.** The Apple ID screen appears.

3. **Tap iCloud to open the iCloud settings.**
4. **Tap Manage Storage.** The iCloud Storage screen appears and displays a list of the items in your iCloud storage as well as how much space each item takes up, as shown in Figure 10.5.

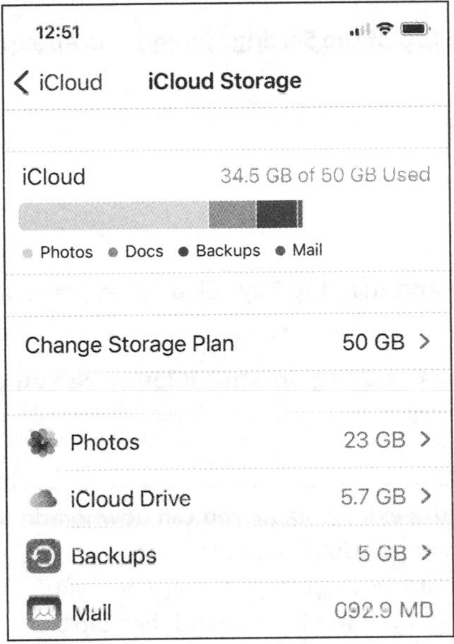

10.5 The Manage Storage screen shows you how much space each item takes up.

5. **To remove data from iCloud, tap an item and then use the following techniques:**
   - **Your iPhone backups.** Tap Delete Backup to remove the current backup.
   - **Other device backups.** Tap Delete Backup to remove the current backup.
   - **Individual documents.** Swipe left on the document, tap the Delete button that appears, and then tap Delete when iOS asks you to confirm.
   - **All documents.** Tap Delete Documents & Data and then tap Delete to confirm.

Changing your iCloud storage plan

If, despite your best management efforts, you find that you're still getting low on iCloud storage, then you should consider changing your storage plan to give yourself more cloud real estate. Follow these steps to upgrade:

1. **In the Home Screen, tap Settings.** The Settings app appears.
2. **Tap your name, which appears at the top of the Settings screen.** The Apple ID screen appears.
3. **Tap iCloud to open the iCloud settings.**
4. **Tap Manage Storage.** The iCloud Storage screen appears.
5. **Tap Change Storage Plan.** The Upgrade iCloud Storage screen appears.
6. **Tap the storage plan you want to use and then tap Buy.** iCloud prompts you for your password.
7. **Type your password, tap OK, and then tap OK again when iCloud tells you the purchase is complete.**

Note

If you find that you're not using the extra storage, you can downgrade to a cheaper plan (or even down to the free 5GB). Follow Steps 1 to 5 to open the Upgrade iCloud Storage screen. Tap Downgrade Options, enter your password, tap Manage, tap the new plan you want to use, and then tap Done.

Upgrading to iCloud Drive

Regular iCloud storage includes backups and email, as well as the documents and data used by individual apps. That's a good feature, but it's limited because it means you can access those documents and the app data only by using the associated apps. In other words, there is no "folder" on iCloud that you can view to see your saved documents and data.

If you'd prefer to see such a folder, as well as use iCloud to save a wider variety of documents and data, then you should consider upgrading to iCloud Drive, which provides all those features and even enables you to access your cloud data from any Mac or PC.

Here are the steps to follow to set up iCloud Drive on your iPhone:

1. **In the Home Screen, tap Settings.** The Settings app appears.
2. **Tap your name, which appears at the top of the Settings screen.** The Apple ID screen appears.

3. **Tap iCloud to open the iCloud settings.**
4. **Tap the iCloud Drive switch to On.** iCloud turns on iCloud Drive and then displays a list of apps that can use iCloud Drive.
5. **For each app that you don't want to store documents in iCloud Drive, tap the app's switch to Off.**

Configuring iCloud on Your Mac

If you want to keep your Mac in sync with the iCloud push services, you need to add your iCloud account to the Mail application and configure iCloud synchronization on your Mac.

Setting up an iCloud account on your Mac

Here are the steps to follow to get your iCloud account into the Mail application:

1. **In the Dock, click the Mail icon.** The Mail application appears.
2. **Choose Mail → Add Account.** Mail displays the Add Account dialog.
3. **Select the iCloud option and click Continue.** The iCloud dialog appears.
4. **Type your Apple ID address and password.**
5. **Click Sign In.** Mail verifies the account info and displays the account summary screen.
6. **Select the check box beside each type of data you want to set up.**
7. **Click Add Account.** Mail adds the iCloud account.

Setting up iCloud synchronization on your Mac

Macs were made to sync with iCloud, so this process should be a no-brainer. To ensure that is the case, you need to configure your Mac to make sure iCloud sync is activated and that your email accounts, contacts, and calendars are part of the sync process. Follow these steps to set your preferences:

1. **Click the System Preferences icon in the Dock.** Your Mac opens the System Preferences window.
2. **Click the iCloud icon.** The first time you do this, your Mac prompts you to sign in to iCloud.

3. **Type your iCloud email address and password, and then click Sign In.** If this is the first time you've launched the iCloud preferences, you run through a few dialogs to set your initial preferences. When that's done, you end up at the iCloud preferences window.
4. **Select the check box beside each data item you want to sync with your iCloud account (see Figure 10.6).**
5. **Click the Close button.** Your Mac is now ready for iCloud syncing.

10.6 Select the check box beside each item you want to sync.

Configuring iCloud on Your Windows PC

iCloud is happy to push data to your Windows PC. However, unlike with a Mac, your Windows machine wouldn't know iCloud if it tripped over it. To get Windows hip to the iCloud thing, you need to follow these steps:

1. **Install the free iCloud app from the Microsoft Store.**

2. **Click Start and then click the iCloud icon.** The iCloud dialog box appears.
3. **Use the Apple ID text box to type your iCloud address.**
4. **Use the Password text box to type your iCloud password.**
5. **Click Sign In.** Windows signs in to your account and then displays the iCloud app, shown in Figure 10.7.
6. **Select the check box beside each type of data you want to sync.**
7. **Click Apply.**

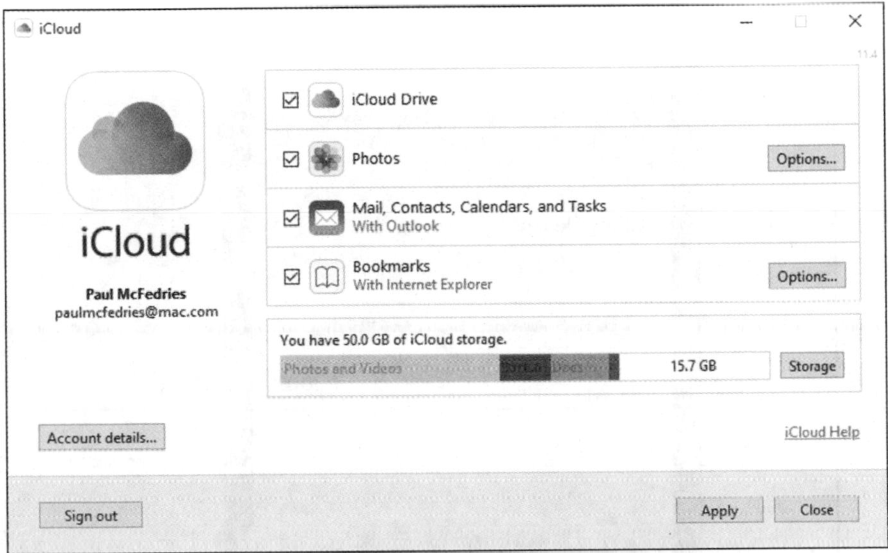

10.7 Use the iCloud app to set up your Windows PC to work with iCloud.

How Do I Fix My iPhone?

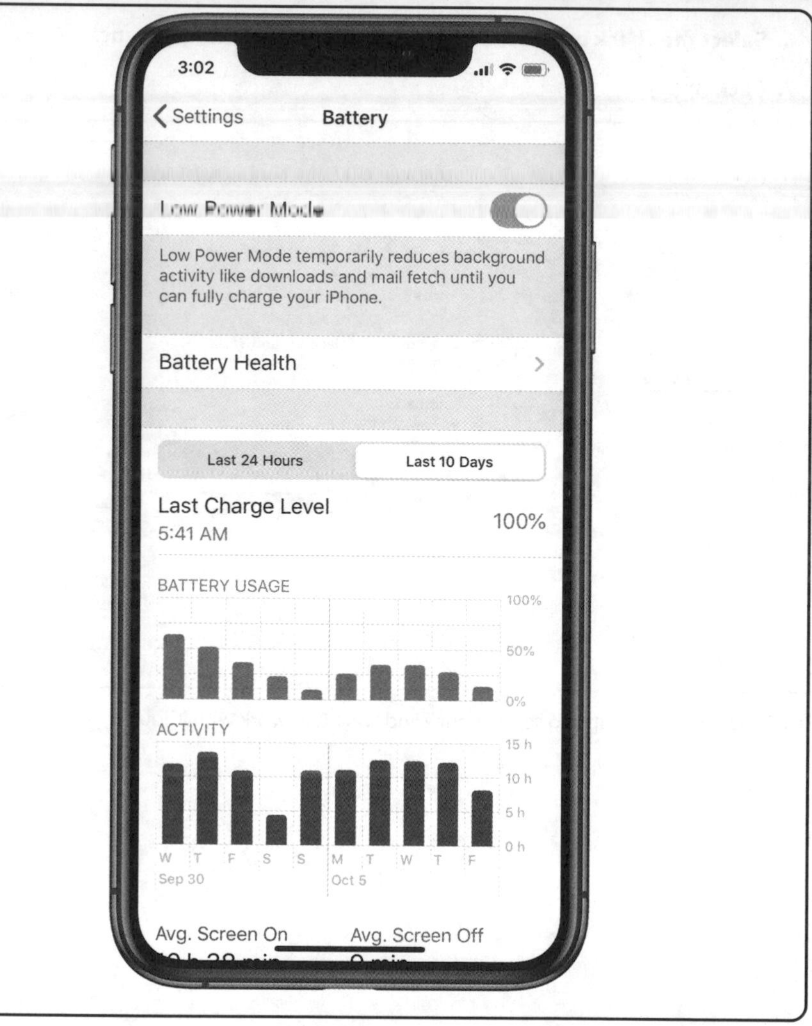

1 2 3 4 5 6 7 8 9 10 11

The good news about iPhone problems — whether they're problems with iPhone software or with the actual iPhone — is that they're relatively rare. On the hardware side, although the iPhone is a sophisticated device that's really a small computer (not just a fancy phone), it's far less complex than a full-blown computer and so much less likely to go south on you. On the software side (and to a lesser extent on the accessories side), app developers (and accessory manufacturers) only have to build their products to work with a single device made by a single company. This really simplifies things, and the result is fewer problems — not, however, zero problems. Even the iPhone sometimes behaves strangely or not at all. This chapter gives you some general troubleshooting techniques for iPhone woes and also tackles a few specific problems.

General Techniques for Troubleshooting Your iPhone

If your iPhone is behaving oddly or erratically, it's possible that a specific component inside the phone is the cause. In that case, you don't have much choice but to ship your iPhone back to Apple for repairs. Fortunately, however, most glitches are temporary and can often be fixed by using one or more of the following techniques:

- **Restart your iPhone.** By far the most common solution to an iPhone problem is to shut it down and then restart it. By rebooting the iPhone, you reload the entire system, which is often enough to solve many problems. You restart your iPhone by pressing and holding both the Side button and either the Volume Up or Volume Down button until you see the Slide to Power Off slider. Drag the Slide to Power Off slider to the right to start the shutdown. When the screen goes completely black, your iPhone is off. To restart, press and hold the Side button until you see the Apple logo and then release the button.
- **Reboot your iPhone hardware.** When you restart your iPhone as I describe in the previous item, what you're really doing is rebooting the system software. If that still doesn't solve the problem, you might need to reboot the iPhone hardware as well. From the Lock screen, press Volume Up, press Volume Down, and then press and hold down the Side button. Keep the button pressed until you see the Apple logo (it takes about 8 seconds or so), which indicates a successful restart.

Genius

The hardware reboot is also the way to go if your iPhone is *really* stuck and holding down both the Side button and one of the Volume buttons doesn't do anything.

- **Recharge your iPhone.** It's possible that your iPhone just has a battery that's completely discharged. Connect your iPhone to your computer or to the Dock. If it powers up and you see the battery logo (this might take a minute or two), then it's charging just fine and will be back on its feet in a while.
- **Shut down a stuck app.** If your iPhone is frozen because an app has gone haywire, you can usually get it back in the saddle by forcing the app to quit. First, display the multitasking screen:
  - If your iPhone has a notch at the top of the screen, slide a finger up from the bottom edge of the screen and then pause about halfway up the screen.

- For all other iPhone models, double-click the Home button (that is, press the Home button twice in succession).

- Now drag the unresponsive app up to the top of the screen to shut down the app.

- **Check for iPhone software updates.** If Apple knows about the problem you're having, it will fix it and then make the patch available in a software update. I tell you how to update your iPhone a bit later in this chapter.

- **Check for app updates.** It's possible that a bug in an app is causing your woes, so you can often solve such problems by updating the app. Fortunately, app updates are automatic in iOS (since version 7), so this should never be much of a problem. To confirm that your apps are updating automatically, open Settings, tap iTunes & App Store, and, in the Automatic Downloads section, make sure the Apps switch is On.

- **Erase and restore your content and settings.** This may seem like drastic advice, but it's possible to perform a complete backup of everything on your iPhone. You can then reset the iPhone to its original, pristine state and then restore the backup. I show you how to back up your iPhone in Chapter 2, and I explain the rather lengthy restore process later in this chapter.

- **Reset your settings.** Sometimes your iPhone goes down for the count because its settings have become corrupted. In that case, you can fix the problem by restoring the iPhone to its original settings. Tap Settings in the Home screen, tap General, tap Reset, and then tap Reset All Settings. When your iPhone asks you to confirm, tap Reset All Settings.

Genius

If resetting your iPhone doesn't get the job done, it could be some recalcitrant bit of content that's causing the problem. In that case, tap Settings in the Home screen, tap General, tap Reset, and then tap Erase All Content and Settings. When your iPhone asks you to confirm, tap Backup Then Erase (which, to be safe, runs an iCloud backup before removing your content and settings).

Troubleshooting connected devices

There are only two ways that you can connect devices to your iPhone: the Lightning connector or Bluetooth. Although the number of devices you can connect is relatively limited, that doesn't mean you might never have problems with those devices.

If you're having trouble with a device attached to your iPhone, the good news is that a fair chunk of those problems have a relatively limited set of causes. You may be able to get the device back on its feet by attempting a few tried-and-true remedies. If it's not immediately obvious what the problem is, then your hardware troubleshooting routine should always start with these very basic techniques:

- **Check connections, power switches, and so on.** Some of the most common (and most embarrassing) causes of hardware problems are the simple physical things, so make sure that a device is turned on and check that cable connections are secure. For example, if you can't access the Internet through the Wi-Fi connection on your iPhone, make sure your network's router is turned on. Also make sure that the cable between your router and the ISP's modem is properly connected.
- **Replace the batteries.** Wireless devices such as headsets really chew through batteries, so if such a device is working intermittently (or not at all), always try replacing the batteries to see whether that solves the problem.
- **Turn the device off and then on again.** You *power cycle* a device by turning it off, waiting a few seconds for its innards to stop spinning, and then turning it back on. You'd be amazed how often this simple procedure can get a device back up and running. For a device that doesn't have an On/Off switch, try either unplugging it from the power outlet or removing and replacing the batteries.
- **Reset the device's default settings.** If you can configure a device, then perhaps some new setting is causing the problem. If you recently made a change, try returning the setting back to its original value. If that doesn't do the trick, most configurable devices have some kind of Restore Default Settings option that enables you to quickly return them to their factory settings.
- **Upgrade the device's firmware.** Some devices come with *firmware* — a small program that runs inside the device and controls its internal functions. For example, all routers have firmware. Check with the manufacturer to see whether a new version exists. If it does, download the new version and then see the device's manual to learn how to upgrade the firmware.

Resetting the iPhone

If you've spent quite a bit of time in the Settings app, your iPhone probably doesn't look much like it did fresh out of the box. That's okay, though, because your iPhone should be as individual as you are. However, if you've gone a bit too far with your customizations, your iPhone might feel a bit alien and uncomfortable. That's okay, too, because there's an easy solution to the problem: You can erase all your customizations and revert the iPhone to its default settings.

A similar problem that comes up is when you want to sell or give your iPhone to someone else. Chances are you don't want the new owner to see your data — contacts, appointments, email and text messages, favorite websites, music, and so on — and it's unlikely the other person wants to wade through all that stuff anyway (no offense). To solve this problem, you can erase not only your custom settings but also all the content you've stored on the iPhone.

The Reset app handles these scenarios and a few more to boot. Here's how it works:

1. **On the Home screen, tap Settings.** The Settings app appears.
2. **Tap General.** The General screen appears.
3. **Scroll to the bottom and tap Reset.** The Reset screen appears.
4. **Tap one of the following reset options:**
   - **Reset All Settings.** Tap this option to reset your custom settings to the factory default settings.
   - **Erase All Content and Settings.** I cover this option in the next section.
   - **Reset Network Settings.** Tap this option to delete your Wi-Fi network settings. This is often an effective way to solve Wi-Fi problems.
   - **Reset Keyboard Dictionary.** Tap this option to reset your keyboard dictionary. This dictionary contains a list of the keyboard suggestions that you've rejected. Tap this option to clear the dictionary and start fresh.

Note

The keyboard dictionary contains those words that your iPhone thought were errors, but you then tapped to use them as is (that is, they're the predictive typed strings that you accepted). For example, if you type "logophile," iPhone suggests "loophole" instead. If you tap the "logophile" predictive typed string to accept it, the word "logophilie" is added to the keyboard dictionary.

   - **Reset Home Screen Layout.** Tap this option to reset your Home screen icons to their default layout.
   - **Reset Location & Privacy.** Tap this option to wipe out the location preferences for your apps. A location warning is the dialog you see when you start a GPS-aware app for the first time. When you start one of these, your iPhone asks if the app can use your current location, and you then tap either Allow or Don't Allow.
5. **When the iPhone asks you to confirm, tap the red button.** Note that the name of this button is the same as the reset option. For example, if you tapped the Reset All Settings option in Step 4, the confirm button is called Reset All Settings. iOS resets the data.

Erasing and restoring data and settings

Sometimes your iPhone goes down for the count because its settings have become corrupted. In that case, you can attempt to fix the problem by restoring iPhone to its original settings. You can then restore your content from an iCloud backup. Follow these steps to erase and restore your iPhone's content and settings:

1. **Update your iPhone to the latest version of iOS.** I describe how to manually update iOS in the next section.
2. **On the Home screen, tap Settings.** The Settings app appears.
3. **Tap General.** The General screen appears.
4. **Scroll to the bottom and tap Reset.** The Reset screen appears.
5. **Tap Erase All Content and Settings.** iOS displays the dialog shown in Figure 11.1.
6. **Tap Backup Then Erase.** If you just made a manual backup, you can tap Erase Now instead. Either way, iOS asks you to confirm that you want to erase your iPhone.
7. **Tap Erase iPhone.** iOS asks you to confirm yet again.
8. **Tap Erase iPhone.** iOS prompts you to enter your Apple ID password.
9. **Type your password and then tap Erase.** At long last, iOS erases your iPhone, restarts the device, and then starts the setup procedure.
10. **Run through the setup procedure to specify settings such as your preferred language, country, and Wi-Fi network.** You eventually end up at the Apps & Data screen.
11. **Tap Restore from iCloud Backup.** iOS prompts you to sign in to iCloud with your Apple ID.
12. **Type your Apple ID email address, tap Next, type your Apple ID password, tap Next, and then tap Agree when the dreaded terms and conditions appear.** The Choose Backup screen appears.
13. **Tap your iPhone's most recent backup.** iOS takes you through a few more setup chores.

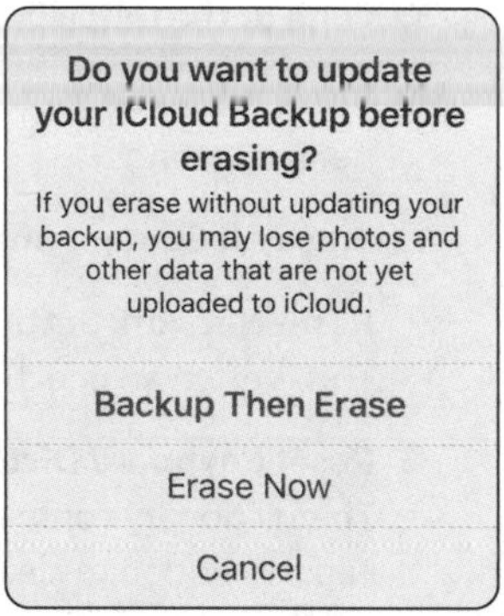

Do you want to update your iCloud Backup before erasing?
If you erase without updating your backup, you may lose photos and other data that are not yet uploaded to iCloud.
Backup Then Erase
Erase Now
Cancel

11.1 You see this dialog when you tap Erase All Content and Settings.

14. **Run through the rest of the setup chores as prompted.** Eventually, you see the Restore from iCloud screen, which shows the progress of the backup restoration. When the restore is complete, iOS loads, and you're back in business.

Updating software

The iPhone software should check for available updates from time to time, provided the phone has an Internet connection. The problem is, you might hear about an important update that adds a feature you're really looking forward to or perhaps fixes a gaping security hole. In that case, you take matters into your own hands and check for updates yourself.

You can check for updates right on your iPhone by following these steps:

1. **On the Home screen, tap Settings.** The Settings app appears.
2. **Tap General.** Your iPhone displays the General options screen.
3. **Tap Software Update.** Your iPhone begins checking for available updates. If you see the message "Your software is up to date," then you can move on to bigger and better things.
4. **If an update is available, tap Download and Install.** Your iPhone downloads the update and then proceeds with the installation, which takes a few minutes.

Caution

Your iPhone goes through with the update only if it has more than 50 percent battery life through the entire update operation. To ensure the update is a success, either plug your iPhone into a power outlet or run the update only when the battery is fully charged.

Taking Care of the iPhone Battery

Your iPhone comes with a large lithium-ion battery that gives you oodles of talk time, Internet use, and audio and video playback. Yes, "oodles" is a vague term. That's because the battery life you get depends on how you use your iPhone, which model you have, the ambient temperature, and the day of week (just kidding on that last one). The biggest downside to the iPhone battery is that it's not, in Apple parlance, *user-installable*. If your battery dies, you have no choice but to return it to Apple to get it replaced. This is all the more reason to take care of your battery and try to maximize its life.

Sending in Your iPhone for Repairs

To have your iPhone repaired, you can either take it to an Apple Store or send it in. Visit www.apple.com/support and follow the prompts to find out how to send in your iPhone for repairs. Remember that the memory comes back wiped, so be sure to make an iCloud backup, if you can. Also, don't forget to remove your SIM card before you send it in.

Tracking battery use

Your iPhone doesn't give a ton of battery data, but you can monitor both the total usage time (this includes all activities: calling, surfing, playing media, and so on) and standby time (time when your iPhone was in Sleep Mode). Also, one of the nice features in iOS is a breakdown of recent battery usage by app, so you can see which apps have been draining your battery. Follow these steps to track your iPhone battery use:

1. **On the Home screen, tap Settings.** The Settings app appears.
2. **Tap Battery.** Your iPhone displays the Battery screen.
3. **Use the charts to view your iPhone's overall battery usage for two time periods: Last 24 Hours and Last 10 Days (see Figure 11.2).**
4. **Use the Battery Usage By App section to view recent usage by app, as shown in Figure 11.2.**

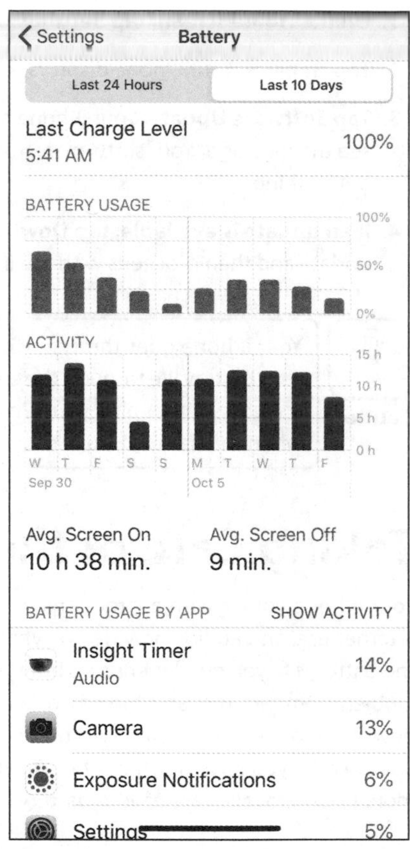

11.2 The Battery screen shows overall battery usage charts and breaks down recent battery usage by app.

Checking battery health

iOS keeps track of your iPhone's overall battery health by tracking two measures:

- **Maximum Capacity.** This is a percentage value that measures your iPhone's current battery capacity (that is, how much power the battery can store at full charge) relative to when the battery was new. A new battery has 100 percent maximum capacity, but that number decreases as the battery ages, so a battery that's a few years old might have a maximum capacity of just 80 percent.
- **Peak Performance Capability.** This is a measure of whether an aging battery is still capable of delivering peak performance. iOS and your iPhone contain special software and hardware systems that attempt to compensate for the reduced performance of older batteries.

To check these measures for your iPhone, follow these steps:

1. **On the Home screen, tap Settings.** The Settings app appears.
2. **Tap Battery.** Your iPhone displays the Battery screen.
3. **Tap Battery Health.** The Battery Health screen appears.
4. **Check out the Maximum Capacity percentage and the message that appears under Peak Performance Capability.**

Here's what to look for:

- If your iPhone battery is new or relatively new, you should see 100% as the Maximum Capacity value and the message "Your battery is currently supporting normal peak performance" under Peak Performance Capability, as shown in Figure 11.3.

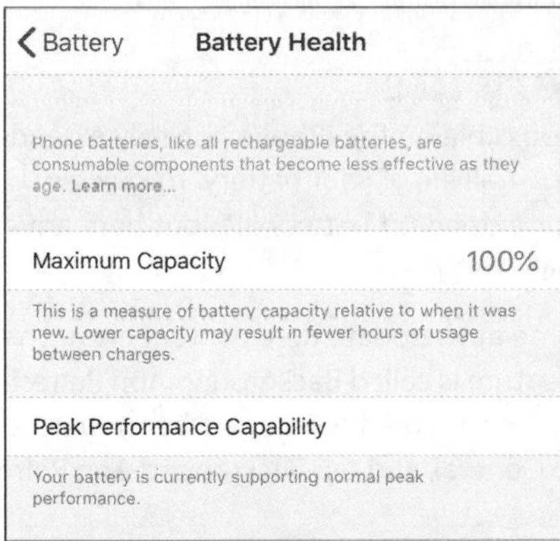

11.3 The Battery Health screen for a relatively new iPhone battery.

- If your iPhone battery is older, you'll see a value less than 100% as the Maximum Capacity value. If your battery can no longer sustain peak performance, even with software and hardware assistance, you see the message "Your battery's health is significantly degraded, and peak performance may be impacted" under Peak Performance Capability, as shown in Figure 11.4. Translation? Time for a new battery!

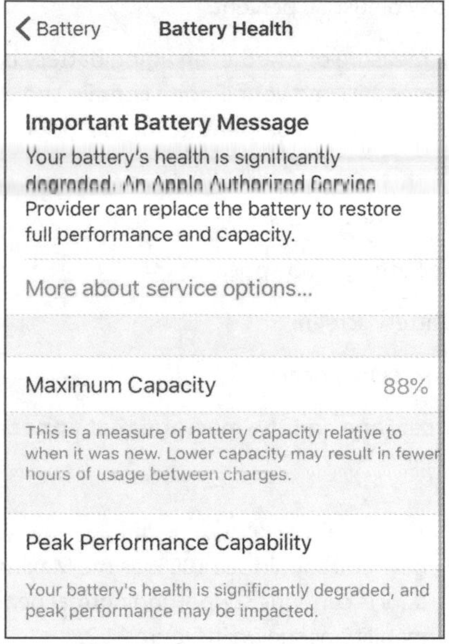

11.4 The Battery Health screen for an older iPhone battery.

Tips for extending battery life

Reducing battery consumption as much as possible on the iPhone not only extends the time between charges but also extends the overall life of your battery. The Battery Usage screen usually offers a suggestion or two for extending battery life, but here are a few suggestions you're not likely to see on that screen:

- **Turn off Background App Refresh.** Some apps update their content even when you're not using them, and this handy feature is called Background App Refresh. Handy, yes, but also a major battery hog, so turn off this feature when you need to go easy on the juice. Open Settings, tap General, and tap Background App Refresh. You have two choices here:

- To disallow all background updates, tap Background App Refresh and then tap Off.
- To disallow background updates for individual apps (particularly active apps such as Facebook and Gmail), tap the app's switch to Off.

- **Turn on Low Power Mode.** This mode saves battery life by turning off Background App Refresh, Mail push, and automatic content and app downloads; disabling a few visual effects; and dimming the screen. iOS asks if you want to switch to Lower Power Mode when the battery level falls to 20 percent, as shown in Figure 11.5. (This message also appears when the level falls to 10 percent.) Tap Low Power Mode to activate this feature. To activate Low Power Mode full-time, open Settings, tap Battery, and tap the Low Power Mode switch to On. Note that you can tell when this feature is active by looking at the battery icon, which turns orange during Low Power Mode.

Note

With Low Power Mode on, Settings automatically configures your iPhone to auto-lock in 30 seconds *and* it disables the Auto-Lock setting.

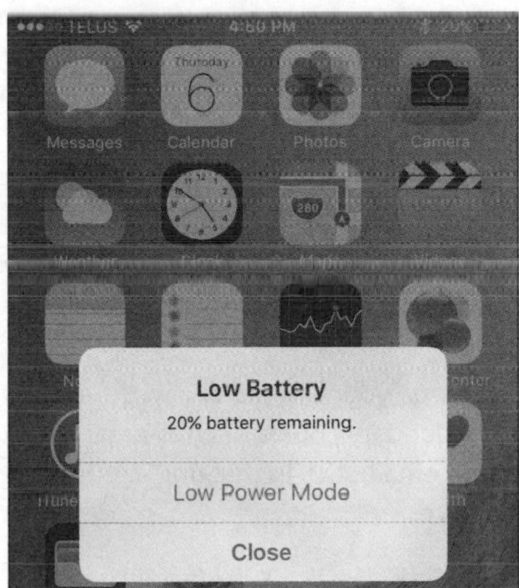

11.5 When your iPhone's battery level falls to 20 percent, iOS asks if you want to switch to Low Power Mode.

- **Dim the screen.** The touchscreen drains a lot of battery power, so dimming it reduces the amount of power used. Either display the Control Center or open Settings and tap Display & Brightness. Then drag the Brightness slider to dim the screen.
- **Cycle the battery.** All lithium-based batteries slowly lose their charging capacity over time. If you can run your iPhone on batteries for four hours today, later you'll only be able to run it for three hours on a full charge. You can't stop this process, but you can delay it significantly by periodically cycling the iPhone battery. *Cycling* — also called *reconditioning* or *recalibrating* — a battery means letting it completely discharge and then fully recharging it again. To maintain optimal performance, you should cycle your iPhone battery every one or two months.

Note

Paradoxically, the less you use your iPhone, the *more* often you should cycle its battery. If you often go several days or a week or two (I can't imagine!) without using your iPhone, then you should cycle its battery at least once a month.

- **Slow the auto-check on your email.** Having your email frequently poll the server for new messages eats up your battery. Set it to check every hour or, ideally, set it to Manual check if you can. To do this, open Settings, tap Mail, tap Accounts, tap Fetch New Data, and then in the Fetch section, tap either Hourly or Manually.
- **Turn off push.** If you have an iCloud or Exchange account, consider turning off the push feature to save battery power. Open Settings, tap Mail, tap Accounts, and then tap Fetch New Data. In the Fetch New Data screen, tap the Push switch to Off, and in the Fetch section, tap Manually.
- **Minimize your tasks.** If you won't be able to charge your iPhone for a while, avoid background chores, such as playing music, or secondary chores, such as organizing your contacts. If your only goal is to read all your email, stick to that until it's done because you don't know how much time you have.
- **Put your iPhone into Sleep Mode manually, if necessary.** If you are interrupted — for example, the pizza delivery guy shows up on time — don't wait for your iPhone to put itself to sleep because those few minutes use precious battery time. Instead, put your iPhone to sleep manually right away by pressing the Side button.

- **Avoid temperature extremes.** Exposing your iPhone to extremely hot or cold temperatures reduces the long-term effectiveness of the battery. Try to keep your iPhone at a reasonable temperature.
- **Turn off Wi-Fi if you don't need it.** When Wi-Fi is on, it regularly checks for available wireless networks, which drains the battery. If you don't need to connect to a wireless network, turn off Wi-Fi to conserve energy. Tap Settings, tap Wi-Fi, and then tap the Wi-Fi switch to Off.
- **Turn off cellular data if you don't need it.** Your iPhone constantly looks for nearby cellular towers to maintain the signal, which can use up battery power in a hurry. If you're surfing on a Wi-Fi network, you don't need cellular data, so turn it off. Tap Settings, tap Cellular, and then tap the Cellular Data switch to Off.
- **Turn off GPS if you don't need it.** When GPS is on, the receiver exchanges data with the GPS system regularly, which uses up battery power. If you don't need the GPS feature for the time being, turn off the GPS antenna. Tap Settings, tap Privacy, tap Location Services, and then tap the Location Services switch to Off.
- **Turn off Bluetooth if you don't need it.** When Bluetooth is running, it constantly checks for nearby Bluetooth devices, and this drains the battery. If you aren't using any Bluetooth devices, turn off Bluetooth to save energy. Tap Settings, tap Bluetooth, and then tap the Bluetooth switch to Off.

Genius

If you don't need all four of the iPhone antennae for a while, a faster way to turn them off is to switch your iPhone to Airplane Mode. Either tap Settings and then tap the Airplane Mode switch to On or open the Control Center and then tap the Airplane Mode icon.

Solving Specific Problems

The generic troubleshooting and repair techniques that you've seen so far can solve all kinds of problems. However, there are always specific problems that require specific solutions. The rest of this chapter takes you through a few of the most common of these problems.

The iPhone screen won't respond to taps

Every now and then, your iPhone might freeze and no amount of tapping, swiping, or threatening will get the phone to respond. The most likely problem is that the touchscreen has become temporarily stuck. To fix that, press the Sleep/Wake button to put the iPhone to sleep, press Sleep/Wake again to wake the iPhone, and then drag Slide to Unlock. In most cases, you should now be able to resume normal iPhone operations.

If that doesn't work, then it's possible that the app you're using has crashed, so you need to shut it down as I describe earlier in the "General Techniques for Troubleshooting Your iPhone" section.

Your battery won't charge

If you find that your battery won't charge, here are some possible solutions:

- **If the iPhone is plugged in to a computer to charge via the USB port, it may be that the computer has gone into standby.** Waking the computer should solve the problem.
- **The USB port might not be transferring enough power.** For example, the USB ports on most keyboards and hubs don't offer much in the way of power. If you have your iPhone plugged in to a USB port on a keyboard or hub, plug it in to a USB port on your Mac or PC.
- **Attach the USB cable to the USB power adapter and then plug the adapter in to an AC outlet.**
- **Double-check all connections to make sure everything is plugged in properly.**
- **Try another Lightning cable if you have one.**

If you can't seem to locate the problem after these steps, you may need to send your iPhone in for service.

You have trouble accessing a Wi-Fi network

Wireless networking adds a whole new set of potential snags to your troubleshooting chores because of problems such as interference and device ranges. Here's a list of a few troubleshooting items that you should check to solve any wireless connectivity problems you're having with your iPhone:

- **Make sure the Wi-Fi antenna is on.** Tap Settings, tap Wi-Fi, and then tap the Wi-Fi switch to On.

- **Make sure the iPhone isn't in Airplane Mode.** Tap Settings and then tap the Airplane Mode switch to Off.
- **Check the connection.** The iPhone has a tendency to disconnect from a nearby Wi-Fi network for no apparent reason. Tap Settings. If the Wi-Fi setting shows as Not Connected, tap Wi-Fi, and then tap your network in the list.
- **Renew the lease.** When you connect to a Wi-Fi network, the access point gives your iPhone a Dynamic Host Control Protocol (DHCP) lease that allows it to access the network. You can often solve connectivity problems by renewing that lease. Tap Settings, tap Wi-Fi, and then tap the blue More Info icon to the right of the connected Wi-Fi network. Tap the DHCP tab and then tap the Renew Lease button, shown in Figure 11.6.

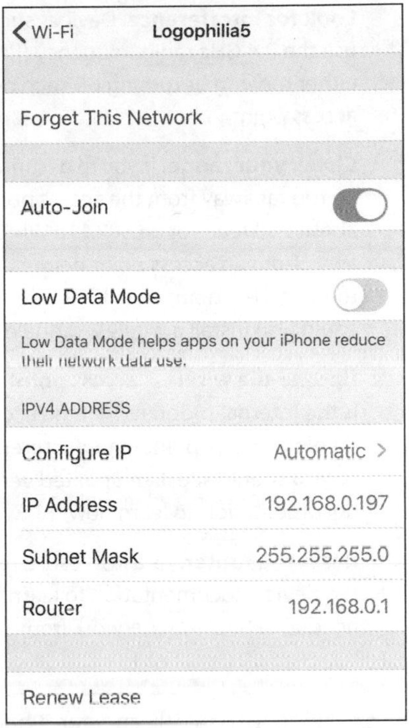

11.6 Open the connected Wi-Fi network settings and then tap Renew Lease to get a fresh lease on your Wi-Fi life.

- **Reconnect to the network.** You can often solve Wi-Fi network woes by disconnecting from the network and then reconnecting. Tap Settings, tap Wi Fi, and then tap the blue More Info icon to the right of the connected Wi-Fi network. Tap Forget This Network (see Figure 11.6) to disconnect and then reconnect to the same network.
- **Reset the network settings on your iPhone.** This removes all stored network data and resets everything to the factory state, which might solve the problem. Tap Settings, tap General, tap Reset, and then tap Reset Network Settings. When your iPhone asks you to confirm, tap Reset Network Settings.
- **Reboot and power cycle devices.** Reset your hardware by performing the following tasks, in order: Restart your iPhone, reboot your iPhone hardware, power cycle the wireless access point, and power cycle the broadband modem.

- **Look for interference.** Devices such as baby monitors and cordless phones that use the 2.4 GHz radio frequency (RF) band can play havoc with wireless signals. Try either moving or turning off such devices if they're near your iPhone or wireless access point.
- **Check your range.** If you're getting no signal or a weak signal, your iPhone could be too far away from the access point. You usually can't get much farther than about 230 feet (for an 802.11n Wi-Fi network; 115 feet for 802.11a/b/g networks) away from an access point before the signal begins to degrade. Either move closer to the access point or, if it has one, turn on the access point's range booster. You could also install a wireless range extender.
- **Update the wireless access point firmware.** The wireless access point firmware is the internal program that the access point uses to perform its various chores. Wireless access point manufacturers frequently update their firmware to fix bugs, so you should see if an updated version of the firmware is available. See your device documentation to learn how this works.
- **Reset the router.** As a last resort, reset the router to its default factory settings (see the device documentation to learn how to do this). Note that if you do this, you need to set up your network from scratch.

Caution

You should keep your iPhone and wireless access point well away from microwave ovens, which can jam wireless signals.

An app is taking up a large amount of space

The iPhone is so useful and so much fun, it's easy to forget that it has limitations, especially when it comes to storage. 64GB sounds like a lot of space, but it can fill up in a hurry if you stuff your iPhone with movies, TV shows, tons of music, and endless photos and videos.

You can tell how much free space your iPhone has left by tapping Settings, then General, and then iPhone Storage. The iPhone Storage screen not only shows you how much storage space you have available but also shows how much space each app is using, as shown in Figure 11.7.

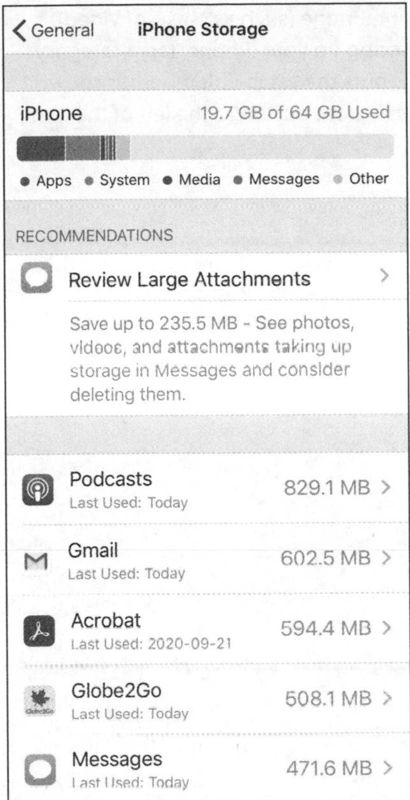

11.7 The iPhone Storage screen tells you how much space each app is taking up.

If you see that your iPhone is running low on space, check the apps to see if any of them are taking up more than their fair share of hard drive real estate. If you see a hard drive hog, you have three ways to give your iPhone some room to breathe:

- **All apps.** Tap the app, tap Offload App, and then tap Offload App when iOS asks you to confirm. This method essentially moves the app itself to the cloud while keeping the app's data on your iPhone.
- **Third-party apps.** For an app you picked up via the App Store, tap the app, tap Delete App, and then tap Delete App when iOS asks you to confirm.

- **Built-in apps.** For an app that came with your iPhone (such as Music or Video), tap the app to display a list of the data it's storing on your iPhone, tap a category (if the app offers any), and then tap Edit. This puts the list in Edit mode, as shown in Figure 11.8. To remove an item, tap the red Delete button to the left of the item, and then tap the Delete button that appears.

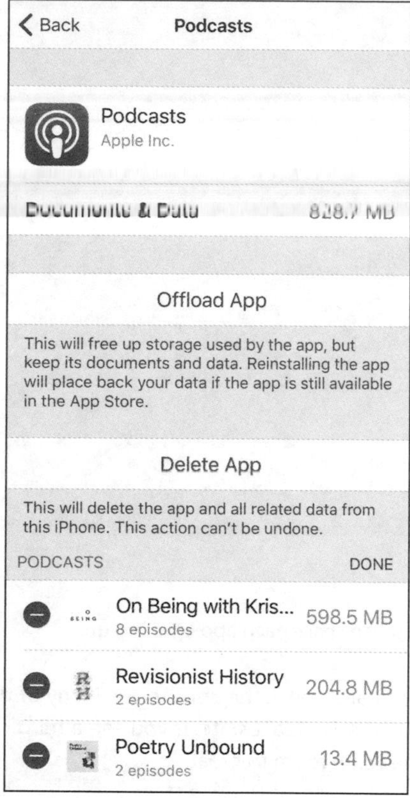

11.8 You can free up storage space by deleting individual items from some of the built-in apps.

Index

A

B

C

D

I

K

L

M

R

S

U

V

W

Y

Z